Rocking
the Roles

Building a Win-Win Marriage

Rocking
the Roles

Robert Lewis and
William Hendricks

NAVPRESS
BRINGING TRUTH TO LIFE
P.O. Box 35001, Colorado Springs, Colorado 80935

"While some choose to acquiesce to modern redefinitions of male-female roles, and others hang on to worn assumptions forged from prejudice, *Rocking the Roles* compels both sides to think again. Lewis and Hendricks have created a 'must read' for every ordained person and every couple who have exchanged sacred vows."

TIM KIMMEL
Author of *Legacy of Love* and
Little House on the Freeway

"This book will challenge your assumptions about traditional marriage."

DENNIS RAINEY, Director of Family Life Ministries
Author of *Building Your Mate's Self-Esteem* and
Lonely Husbands, Lonely Wives

The Navigators is an international Christian organization. Our mission is to reach, disciple, and equip people to know Christ and to make Him known through successive generations. We envision multitudes of diverse people in the United States and every other nation who have a passionate love for Christ, live a lifestyle of sharing Christ's love, and multiply spiritual laborers among those without Christ.

NavPress is the publishing ministry of The Navigators. NavPress publications help believers learn biblical truth and apply what they learn to their lives and ministries. Our mission is to stimulate spiritual formation among our readers.

© 1991, 1998 by Robert Lewis and William Hendricks
All rights reserved. No part of this publication may be reproduced in any form without written permission from NavPress, P.O. Box 35001, Colorado Springs, CO 80935.
Library of Congress Catalog Card Number: 98-33948
ISBN 1-57683-125-6

Cover design by Design Works

Some of the anecdotal illustrations in this book are true to life and are included with the permission of the persons involved. All other illustrations are composites of real situations, and any resemblance to people living or dead is coincidental.

Unless otherwise identified, all Scripture quotations in this publication are taken from the *New American Standard Bible* (NASB), © The Lockman Foundation 1960, 1962, 1963, 1968, 1971, 1972, 1973, 1975, 1977. Another version used is the *HOLY BIBLE: NEW INTERNATIONAL VERSION* ® (NIV®). Copyright © 1973, 1978, 1984 by International Bible Society. Used by permission of Zondervan Publishing House. All rights reserved.

Printed in the United States of America

3 4 5 6 7 8 9 10 / 08 07 06 05 04 03

FOR A FREE CATALOG OF
NAVPRESS BOOKS & BIBLE STUDIES,
CALL 1-800-366-7788 (USA)
OR 1-416-499-4615 (CANADA)

Contents

PREFACE   11
   1. Modern-Day Dilemma   13

PART ONE: ROLE CHAOS
   2. The Myth of the Roleless Marriage   21
   3. Why the Roleless Marriage Won't Work   27
   4. Reflections on the Traditional Family   33
   5. Searching for the Biblical Ideal   41

PART TWO: THE HUSBAND'S CORE ROLE
   6. The High Calling of Headship   53
   7. Lording Leader or Serving Leader?   61
   8. Twenty-Five Ways to Be a Servant-Leader   69

PART THREE: THE HUSBAND'S CORE CONCERNS
   9. Feminine Understanding   77
  10. What Every Wife Needs to Succeed   81

PART FOUR: THE WIFE'S CORE ROLE
  11. What's a Woman to Choose?   91
  12. Husband-Lover and Child-Lover   97

PART FIVE: THE WIFE'S CORE CONCERNS
13. Getting into a Man's Head   107
14. What Every Wife Needs to Know
    About Her Husband   113
15. What Every Husband Needs to Succeed   119
16. What Else a Husband Needs to Succeed   125

PART SIX: RESPONSES THAT ENERGIZE THE ROLES
17. The "S" Word   135
18. The Masculine Counterpart to the "S" Word   145

PART SEVEN: PROBLEMS AND SOLUTIONS
19. Common "Head"-Aches   155
20. Is There Hope for the Headless Family?   163
21. "Helper" Doesn't Mean "Enabler"   169
22. The Church: Can It Be a Refuge for Women?   175
23. Church Intervention: A Case Study   183

PART EIGHT: PRACTICAL APPLICATIONS
24. Forget-Me-Nots   191
25. Seasons of Life   199
26. Gifting Your Child's Marriage   207
27. New Life for Your Marriage!   217

APPENDIX
   I. Roleless Chaos of Another Day   223
  II. Paul's Fresh Alternative   231

Questions and Answers   235
Endnotes   249

To
Sherard
My gift from God . . .
My tranquility in the tempest . . .
My soul mate in the journey . . .
My wife.

Preface

This is a book about roles in marriage. That being the case, you may find it odd when you turn to chapter 1 that I begin with a marriage in which the couple has tried to do away with roles. But it's no surprise really; the trend among married couples today is to downplay, if not eliminate, clearly defined roles. Is that a helpful development? Not really. The roleless ideal sounds noble, but it fails to deliver on its bright promises. It usually ends up in chaos.

Marital chaos is the subject of part 1. Whether we're talking about the roleless marriage of the nineties or the "traditional" family of the fifties, modern couples have had no end of trouble making marriage work. Generations of relational "experts" and self-help gurus have come and gone; yet marriages continue to suffer. What fascinates me—and what I show in part 1—is that no one has paid much attention to the fundamental issue of roles. Roles are like the keel of a ship that lies hidden under cold, dark water, out of sight, out of mind. Yet try sailing without one! In the same way, try building a marriage without clearly defined roles! Part 1 concludes by showing that the Bible has as much to say to marriages in our culture as it did to those of its original readers.

Parts 2 through 5 apply the biblical concept of roles to men and women, respectively. I introduce the concept of "core roles," the essential responsibilities that God gives to a husband or wife.

I also address "core concerns," those primary needs a wise husband and wife will seek to meet in each other.

Then, in part 6, I'll offer a new perspective on that old bugaboo, submission—one that you've probably never heard before.

In part 7, I'll talk about the abuses that occur in marriage when couples fail to understand these primary functions.

Part 8 deals with some issues that we must consider in light of biblical roles in marriage.

The questions at the end of each part are meant for husbands and wives to discuss together. Groups of married or engaged couples can also adapt the questions for group discussion. Group leaders might ask husbands and wives to share their answers with each other first, then share with the larger group their general insights. Or couples might study questions alone before the group meeting, deciding which insights they feel comfortable sharing with the larger group. Encourage husbands and wives to respect their spouses and not to break confidences to the larger group. Also, these questions don't have to be done in one sitting. Spread them out over several weeks or months; don't move on until you feel comfortable with where the discussions end. However you use these questions—as a couple or in a group of couples—be sure to close each time with prayer, asking God to help you apply what you're discovering together.

Finally, the book ends with an Appendix that examines a historical/scriptural perspective on roles in marriages, and a section of questions and answers on matters that I am frequently asked about whenever I present the material in this book.

I want to emphasize that roles are absolutely critical in marriage. The subject may lack the emotional appeal of topics like commitment and trust, fathers and sons, finances and debt, or intimacy and sex. But I've discovered that so many of the "felt needs" of couples and families today find their roots in the toxic soil of chaotic roles. Surely the fastest way out of trouble is to re-plant the relationship on solid, healthy ground, and rediscover the design of the Creator who made us in His image—male and female He created us.

Let's begin, then, on a rainy afternoon at Debbie's house . . .

1

Modern-Day Dilemma

Debbie enjoyed the cry of the teakettle. Its pure, solitary note reminded her that she was alone. Husband away. Kids off to school. A rare day to herself. No commute. No errands. No commitments. She almost felt guilty for owning the next few hours.

Not too guilty. Debbie knew she deserved this moment, however brief. Teacup in hand, she folded her legs under her, catlike, on the sofa, tucked an afghan around her, and squeezed out the last chill of the November rain outside.

On a shelf before her paraded the family's history: photographs of her grandparents, her parents on their wedding day, her own wedding portraits with John, a family reunion, John's mother and brother, his father as a boy, John graduating from business school, baby pictures of her children—Jennifer and Jason— and a snapshot of the children proudly displaying their best attempts at a sand castle on their first visit to the seashore. As her eyes panned across these frames, she found herself thinking of how she might rearrange the collection next week, when she would add a family portrait taken last month.

Suddenly waves of weariness began to wash over her. She felt very old—and very rushed with her life. She felt confused, and disappointed. Life was not working out quite the way she and John had planned. She wondered why.

She had met John in one of those happy collisions that give credence to the belief that marriages are made in heaven. She was an entry-level writer at a public relations firm. He was a graduate student hired at slave wages to keep the company's books. They discovered each other one evening when, having stayed late to complete assignments, both independently ordered out for Chinese food. The two dinners arrived simultaneously, and for a moment, confusion reigned. But soon, meals were mingled with a lengthy conversation in the company kitchen, and that irresistible chemistry called love took root.

They married late the next summer, before John started classes again. By then, Debbie had moved to another agency. Her salary was adequate to support them both. She actually took pleasure from the idea that she was "putting her husband through" business school.

The investment paid off. Upon graduation John was hired by a major accounting firm — into a fast track leading to upper management. He announced the good news over a meal of (what else?) Chinese food, talking in rapid succession about the position and its opportunities, about the company and its advantages, about moving to a new city and being able to buy their first house, about. . . .

A storm cloud had suddenly drenched the parade. Doubt, even panic, flew like knives from Debbie's eyes. He asked what was the matter. She told him. Well, yes, he guessed she would have to quit her job. But hey, it wasn't like they were moving to a ghost town; there would surely be plenty of jobs for a person of her skills and experience, blah, blah, blah. She thought he sounded like . . . well, like a publicity agent trying to put the best possible face on a bad deal.

The conflict had led to a long discussion over *marriage* roles, of all things. How old-fashioned the term sounded, like a relic from their parents' generation. But now, suddenly, it dominated the discussion, which moved far beyond the issue of relocation, to paychecks and income sharing, housework and chores, timing and number of children, who would "raise" the kids, vacations, investments, religion, romance, sex, and ten thousand other chasms across which bridges must be built.

One thing Debbie knew for certain—she did *not* want a role arrangement like that of her parents. Fran always deferred to Harold's whims and wishes. Her mother was no weak, passive woman. Indeed, through a thousand subtle stratagems she ran the home and kept the family together. Yet she had allowed her husband to enjoy the illusion of ruling as king in his castle. Debbie never understood why. Such a relationship repulsed her.

In her own marriage, Debbie wanted to do it clean. And John concurred. Since his parents were separated when he was eight and divorced when he was fourteen, he felt that he brought an enlightened neutrality to any discussion of marital roles. So together they declared theirs to be a "marriage of equality." Both partners would be able to pursue their career of choice (even though John's announcement had already challenged that ideal). They agreed that the next time a question of relocation arose, they would sit down and decide together whose career should take precedence.

As for housework and chores, they would split them fifty-fifty. They even drew up a list and volunteered for the various tasks. (Even though John ended up with most of the financial matters and the upkeep of the cars, while Debbie was to oversee most of the housecleaning and shopping, they were satisfied that fairness, not stereotypes, had decided these issues.)

On the matter of children . . . they would wait and see. Debbie knew she wanted a child—someday—and she knew she would want to stay home with a baby for at least the first two years. John claimed neutrality on the point. Whatever she wanted, that was fine with him, as long as she was happy. He surely wasn't going to tell her what to do.

For a time, he didn't. After moving to the new city, John threw himself into his job with enviable ambition. Debbie took a position with an advertising firm. They worked hard. They made money. They made friends. They went out to dinner. They bought a house. They spent weekends at the beach. Before long they received promotions. John began traveling. Debbie began managing her own accounts.

Then one evening Debbie announced that her job would require some travel, too. John exploded. And so did the "marriage of equality." He would have none of it, he declared. She would just have to give the accounts to someone else. Or maybe she ought to find a new job.

Shocked at this outburst, Debbie probed for an explanation. Accusations began spilling out: He resented her being so busy. She never had time for him anymore. Her clients saw her more than he did. She wasn't keeping the house clean enough. He was tired of cooking dinner for himself. When were they going to start a family? For that matter, when were they going to have sex again? He wanted a wife, not a business partner.

Debbie's claws extended, and she pounced on him with her own list of wrongs suffered. How dare he criticize her housekeeping, when he littered his path with socks, towels, shirts, shoes, underwear, glasses, wrappers, and magazines? Was he tired of cooking for himself? She was tired of cleaning up his dishes, to say nothing of yard work while he was away, keeping her car serviced, and picking up his shirts at the cleaners. It was he, not she, who neglected conversation in the evenings, coming home like a catatonic zombie, grunting one-word responses to her questions about his day. As for children and their sex life . . . she burst into tears, overcome with frustration, confusion, and rage.

The conversation lasted into the night. Once again they were forced to examine their roles and expectations. It was obvious something was wrong. The ideal had crumbled. This time John introduced the view that a wife should be "available" to her husband. He struggled to describe exactly what he meant by this. But he was certain it didn't include Debbie's traveling all over the country, leaving him at home to fend for himself.

When she pointed out that that was exactly what his own travel meant for her, he demurred. That was, well, different. He was a man. He was a provider. He had to do what he had to do. It wasn't that she couldn't travel. But she was a woman. She was supposed to be more attached to home. Not that she couldn't work. But her job was, well, optional—a matter of choice rather than necessity. After all, she *had* said she expected to have children. And she *had* said she wanted to provide a warm, loving home for them. So shouldn't she begin constructing that nest now? Her body wouldn't wait forever. To him, the logic seemed flawless.

The conversation left Debbie exhausted, angry, and torn. Much of what he said she didn't like. In some ways she felt trapped. Yet in other ways she agreed. Deep down, however, she sensed a fundamental shift in their relationship. Things were no longer "equal." They never had been, really. Perhaps they never could be.

The forces at work in their relationship seemed to be pulling her more and more homeward. A year later she gave birth to Jennifer, two years after that to Jason. She divested herself of her career, throwing her enormous energy into mothering.

By now John was traveling much less, though handling more responsibility. His job paid well—not so well as to offset the loss of Debbie's income, but enough to maintain the family's lifestyle. In exchange, though, the position absorbed his emotional life. Like most of his peers, his sense of himself became one and the same with his career. At home he functioned as a sympathetic—yet detached—husband and father. He kept up his chores by paying yard boys and mechanics to do the work. Occasionally he changed a diaper, emptied the dishwasher, or even vacuumed, but usually with a remark to Debbie about hiring a maid, to which she responded with a gigantic roll of her ocean-blue eyes.

When the kids had both started school, Debbie expressed a desire to return to work. John voiced no objections. Whatever she wanted, that was fine with him. As long as she was happy and (he added) "could manage with the children." He surely wasn't going to tell her what to do.

So Debbie reentered the work force. It wasn't easy. Old contacts had turned over in the decade she'd been away. Employers wanted to see what she'd done *recently*. None of them talked in glowing terms of future opportunities, as they had when she'd been fresh out of college, naive but exuberant—and single. But she persevered and finally persuaded a small firm to take her on.

That was two years ago. Since then her life had become a comet, blazing in its boomerang orbit around home and work, always in motion, always on the go, never at rest. Yet now, with her cup of tea and the soft sounds of the rain outside, rest felt so good. She had been avoiding rest. To rest was to feel. To feel was to know the ache of resentment she felt toward John and the betrayal she felt toward herself. She had wanted anything but a traditional marriage arrangement. Yet ironically her mother, who had one, seemed to enjoy far more happiness and contentment than she. So much for a "marriage of equality." Her relationship with John was hardly equal, and now it was far from satisfying. Yet what alternatives did she have? What hope was there for marriage and life to be any different?

As the rain slowed down and finally stopped, the house sat still and silent.

Part One
ROLE CHAOS

2

The Myth of the Roleless Marriage

I can assure you that Debbie and John never intended to end up where they are. They are bright, talented people who have a lot going for them. But I fear for their marriage. It seems headed for real trouble. They are up against forces that are far more powerful, complex, and deep-seated than they can possibly imagine. In this chapter we'll discover what some of those forces are.

But first, what about you? What do the roles look like in your marriage? Are you satisfied with the part you play? Maybe you follow a "traditional" pattern and wonder why anyone would want something different. Maybe you started out that way, but now you're caught in what a friend of mine calls the "Little House on the Freeway"!

Or maybe, like Debbie and John, you and your spouse hold out hope of achieving "equality" in your relationship. Ideally, you both intend to pursue careers that make the best use of your skills and bring you maximum fulfillment — along with two incomes. In parenting, you both intend to bring up baby, partners together in feedings, diaper changes, bedtime stories, baths, first steps, and the like. Household tasks you'll split fifty-fifty, or close to it, or else combine forces to complete the tasks. As for decisions, you'll both have a say, working together to negotiate a consensus instead of either one dominating the outcome. In these and a hundred other areas, you'll strive for democracy in your relationship. You'll try to preserve each other's dignity, and respect each other's autonomy. You'll move ahead together in a complementary, noncompetitive, mutually supportive way.

OZZIE AND HARRIET ARE GONE

These are the ideals of countless couples today. Very few would claim to have mastered them. Yet without question, the vision of an egalitarian, roleless marriage has become extraordinarily popular during the last twenty years. As one young woman expressed it to a *Time* magazine reporter, "I intend to be married to someone who will share all the responsibilities."[1]

Those of us who are older and more cynical may smile. But the egalitarian ideal has grown so pervasive and powerful in our society that the older, more "traditional" form of marriage is now considered by many to be unacceptable—and quite possibly on its way to extinction. Intact families with Mom, Dad, and the kids represented only 32 percent of all United States households in 1980; by 1990, the number fell to 27 percent.[2]

Furthermore, in the last two decades the dual-income family has become the norm. Unthinkable by some even twenty years ago, it is now a virtual obligation that a wife develops her own career. "Of course we will work," a twenty-one-year-old college senior says of her generation of future wives. "What are we going to do? Stay at home? When I get married, I expect to contribute 50 percent of my family's income."[3]

Her expectations about working outside the home are shared by a majority of married couples with children today. Almost two-thirds of them—16 million families—had two incomes in 1988. In 8 million of those households, both husband and wife are employed full-time, year-round.[4] In more than 20 percent of the dual-earner couples in the United States in 1997, wives earn more than husbands.[5]

Is the increase of dual-income couples a positive trend? Not if you feel any loyalty toward a "traditional" family structure. *Miami Herald* columnist Charles Whited lamented,

> Much of women's so-called "liberation," meaning going out into the work place to earn livings and support families, has been forced by circumstance or abandonment. And this has opened a whole Pandora's Box of social consequences. . . . We've lost something between the sexes that used to be near and dear, that bonded, strengthened and made life worth living. I'm not sure that we can afford the loss.[6]

Likewise, Gary Bauer, former White House advisor on the family, warned of:

> The risk that loving husbands and wives who read and hear that they represent an insignificant minority will begin to question their decisions to forego extra income and material possessions in order to devote themselves to the raising of children. These are the very people we should be affirming

for their sacrificial contributions to the future of our nation. That fact was widely understood until recent years.[7]

Maybe so. But our culture has probably passed the point of no return in its acceptance—at least in principle—of the egalitarian, roleless marriage. Even if very few couples ever achieve that ideal, fewer still would ever return to the family of the fifties. Ozzie and Harriet are indeed gone forever.

THE MYTH OF THE ROLELESS MARRIAGE

I for one am shedding no tears over the demise of the fifties family. I'll explain why later. In the meantime, I have grave doubts about the new alternative that so many are promoting today—the roleless marriage, the marriage of equality that Debbie and John started out with. Despite twenty or more years of positive press and experimentation with that model, couples don't appear any closer to achieving "equality" in their relationships than before. Instead, I find a lot of confusion, heartbreak, frustration, and denial.

In fact, the egalitarian marriage is little more than a myth. Take housework, for instance. If you want to find out who is "equal" in a marriage, housework is a good place to start. Anybody can get excited about paid employment. But what happens when there's work to do that doesn't involve pay, like household chores? In the roleless marriage, you'd expect these to be split fifty-fifty. Yet twenty-five years of research on who does the chores shows that employed married women work

> roughly fifteen hours longer each week than men. Over a year, they [work] an extra month of twenty-four-hour days a year [sic]. Over a dozen years, it [is] an extra year of twenty-four-hour days. Most women without children spend much more time than men on housework; with children, they devote more time to both housework and childcare.[8]

How much more is "more" for these women? Eighty percent (!) of the household chores, according to a recent Rand Corporation study. Researchers also discovered that when a husband does take on more housework, he tends to assume the chores done by the children rather than by the wife.[9] As one wife says, "When we first got married, we discussed how we would try and keep the housework at a fifty-fifty split. That lasted until the house needed to be cleaned."[10] Her frustration is not uncommon; the failure of husbands to help with household chores was second only to money as a cause of resentment in a nationwide Roper poll of women's changing attitudes toward men.[11]

In short, employed wives not only handle the responsibilities of a job outside the home, but work what sociologist Arlie Hochschild calls a "second shift" once they arrive home. In a celebrated study of fifty dual-income families, she found that only 20 percent split chores and child-rearing equally. Surprisingly, it was the "traditional" husbands who pitched in to help more than the "transitional" ones—men who were all for their wives' employment.[12] In fact, these latter couples often created a "family myth" to rationalize their unequal arrangement. For instance: "We aren't competing over who will take responsibility at home; we're just dreadfully busy with our careers."[13]

SOME ARE MORE EQUAL THAN OTHERS

Are current trends any improvement over the Ozzie-and-Harriet homes of the fifties and sixties? Hardly! It seems women have lost ground, not gained it. They not only have to keep house; they have to help pay for it as well! And supposedly this is an equal arrangement. It reminds me of the thought in George Orwell's *Animal Farm* that we're all equal, but some are more equal than others.[14]

Think back to Debbie and John. They wanted to get beyond the chauvinism and inequities that they had seen perpetuated in traditional marriages. I've met scores of couples like them, pursuing the same goal. They've tried to ignore, or at least minimize, gender distinctions and stereotypical roles. Yet time after time, they've fallen short of this ideal, just as Debbie and John have. Despite their best efforts, their marriages end up in quasitraditional patterns, or else dissolve altogether.

That seems odd to me. If the roleless marriage is such an

improvement over the traditional one, why are so few couples having success with it? Why does it fail to deliver on its bright promise of equality? Why do so many couples eventually slip back into more traditional patterns?

I believe the roleless marriage doesn't work in real life because it *can't* work. It's a fundamentally flawed concept, no matter how appealing it may sound in theory. In the next chapter I'll give three reasons why.

3
Why the Roleless Marriage Won't Work

"This is a transitional generation, in the middle of changing values and roles," said one respected career consultant and columnist. "Each couple is forced to make it up by themselves."[1] I don't know about "forced," but many couples trying to write their own script are swinging the pendulum away from clearly defined roles toward an undefined "marriage of equality." I think they are misguided and here are three reasons why.

A Completely Egalitarian Relationship Makes Little Sense Organizationally

Have you ever thought of your marriage as an organization? It is. A simple one, to be sure. And at times it may look pretty *disorganized!* But you have two people in the relationship, so that qualifies as an organization. Like all organizations, there are all kinds of human dynamics and relational forces at work.

But the roleless marriage closes its eyes to that fact. For instance, in a successful organization, members complement rather than imitate one another in their functions. Everyone has his or her task to do. Yet, as we've seen, the roleless marriage tries to reverse that: Both partners are supposed to share everything fifty-fifty.

Let me ask, would you want to work for a company where no one is allowed to "take charge" or accept final responsibility for decisions that are made? Would you want to send your child to a school where there were no designated teachers or principal? Would you live in a country with no government? Of course not! These would not be organizations—they would be disasters!

On the other hand, who would want to be part of a system where *everyone* had to run the company, oversee the school, or handle the government? Again, there would be more *disorganization* than organization.

Now granted, marriage is a far cry from these examples, in that only two people are involved. Yet the same organizational principles apply. Why ignore them? Only a cruel idealist would demand that you achieve in your marriage a level of equality or sameness that exists nowhere else in human experience.

Marriage is an organization. And like any organization, large or small, it can succeed only by accepting the timeless principle that the partners carry out complementary functions. In other words, marriages work best when the partners have roles.

History and Culture Offer Little Hope for Roleless Relationships

"Each couple is forced to make it up by themselves," the expert said. If that's so, what are the chances of a couple succeeding? Is there any historical precedent for the roleless marriage?

The answer is no. In fact, all the data suggest just the opposite—an extraordinarily consistent pattern in the way men and women relate to one another and in how they divide and handle responsibilities. Looking at a vast body of anthropological and sociological studies, Yale sociologist Stephen Clark reported a consistent arrangement among all known cultures:

> Men bear primary responsibility for the larger community. Women bear primary responsibility for domestic management and rearing of young children. Every known society, past or present, assigns to the men a primary responsibility for the government of the larger groupings within a society, and assigns to the women a primary responsibility for the daily maintenance of the household unit and the care of the younger children.
>
> . . . This general underlying pattern emerges universally.[2]

Dr. Sherry Ortner, a professor of anthropology at the University of Michigan, has spent years studying this issue. Like Stephen Clark, Dr. Ortner found women universally subordinated to men:

> The fact that it [female subordination] exists within every type of social and economic arrangement and in societies of every degree of complexity, indicates to me that we are up against something very profound, very stubborn, something we cannot rout out simply by rearranging a few tasks and roles in the social system, or even by reordering the whole economic structure. . . .
>
> I would flatly assert that we find women subordinated to

men in every known society. The search for a genuinely egalitarian, let alone matriarchal, culture has proved fruitless.[3]

A veritable "horde" of archaeologists and social anthropologists has searched diligently into prehistoric cultures as well as into the present conditions of primitive societies around the world. They have not uncovered a single undisputed case of cultural matriarchy.[4]

Please understand, I'm not saying that I approve of the way cultures have often mistreated women. Nor do I approve of any present injustices toward women. The relevance here is, wherever we turn, *culture* speaks against treating men and women in identical ways. To do so is "unnatural," if history is any guide.

So, if you've attempted to construct a roleless, egalitarian marriage and ended up only in frustration and disillusionment, take heart! All the evidence shows that no other society in the history of the world has ever accomplished it either. Quite the opposite: Every culture assigns distinct roles and a clear division of responsibilities to men and women in marriage.

The Roleless Marriage Contradicts the Plain Teaching of the Bible

Of course, this point is not a problem if you've dismissed the Bible. Nor will it matter if you have no intention of living according to its teaching. But if you believe the Bible to be God's truth, with application for the crucial issues of life — such as marriage — then you'll want to know that there are severe differences between the egalitarian concept and the Bible's teaching on marriage. Let me briefly mention two of these.

First, the Bible is very clear about how marriage should be organized. It uses words like *head, protect,* and *provide* when speaking to husbands, and *helper, lover,* and *submission* when speaking to wives. These words point to distinct roles. I'm going to define these terms in detail later, but the point to be grasped is this: Scripture doesn't blend genders together; it keeps them distinct. The husband is responsible for a specific kind of leadership. Meanwhile, the wife is responsible for a specific kind of support and nurture. These marital duties describe a simple *organizational* arrangement, but one that has proven very effective and stable throughout history.

Second, instead of diminishing gender distinctions, the Bible *insists* on them (Genesis 1:27):

> God created man [i.e. humankind] in His own image . . .
> male and female He created them.

Genesis 2 goes on to describe in detail the creation of Eve as both the complement to Adam and as the final completion of creation. Later, in the New Testament, the apostle Paul cites the creation account as the basis for his differing instructions to husbands and wives. In short, maleness and femaleness mean something very important in the Bible, something nonnegotiable. There's no notion of a unisex, roleless marriage.[5]

THE APPEAL OF THE ROLELESS MARRIAGE

The Bible describes specific roles for husbands and wives, which will be explained in parts 2 through 6 of this book. For now, can you see why Debbie and John's marriage in chapter 1 has not turned out the way they expected? They began with a beautiful ideal, but the concept was structurally flawed. It ignored some basic principles of organizational management. It also overlooked their God-given male and female differences. Sure, before God they are *equal,* but that does not mean they are the *same.* And though they never turned to the Bible to begin with, their view of marriage violated some important biblical principles. Overall, their relationship bears striking testimony to the fact that there are no roleless marriages.

Yet, having said that, let me point out that there is something *very* appealing in Debbie and John's ideal, something we ought to preserve. For all of its flaws, the egalitarian concept of marriage springs, I believe, from a genuine concern to see fairness, justice, and respect operating between married partners. These concepts are biblical, too! God wants to build those qualities into every relationship. I think we all want them. Unfortunately, the roleless marriage doesn't deliver them. And by the way, neither does the traditional marriage.

"But isn't that really what you're advocating—the traditional arrangement?" I hear someone asking. No, I'm not. In this book I want to promote a *biblical* perspective on marriage, not a traditional one. Unfortunately, many people—in fact, most Christians—have come to assume that the traditional marriage *is* the biblical form of marriage. Some Christians advocate that the number-one priority on the church's agenda should be to "get back" to a form of marriage that supposedly existed in the fifties and early sixties.

That would be one of the greatest mistakes we could ever make because that way of marriage was *not* biblical either. It is certainly not the marriage arrangement I would want, and I'm convinced it is not marriage as God intended it. In the next chapter we'll find out why.

4

Reflections on the Traditional Family

What does the "ideal" family look like today? A majority of North Americans have a pretty clear picture of what they would like it to be: a "Leave It to Beaver" model—a father who works while the mother stays home and cares for the two kids. That's what 63 percent of adults in a Gallup survey recently said they'd prefer. Amazing! Only a third would choose a situation in which both parents work and take care of the children equally.[1]

This ideal has come to be known as the traditional family. For some it is the All-American family. Most of us watched it by the hour on that new technological marvel of the fifties, the great engine of socialization—prime-time television. "Leave It to Beaver." "Father Knows Best." "The Adventures of Ozzie and Harriet." "Make Room for Daddy." "The Donna Reed Show." Pure entertainment.

What no one could foresee was the powerful impression these programs would leave on the United States' first TV generation, the postwar baby boomers, those of us in our forties and fifties, now watching as our own children grow up and leave home. Many of us grew up watching these prime-time families. As Gallup's figures indicate, they became a virtual archetype of what "family" was supposed to mean in our country.

THE SACCHARINE SEVEN

Why, then, during the last two decades, have so many of us rejected this traditional model? I suppose any number of complex sociological and psychological theories could be cited to explain its passing. Still, it's hard to beat the simple, pungent wisdom of one of my favorite "theologians," Erma Bombeck. In her book *Motherhood: The Second Oldest Profession,* she has a brilliant chapter entitled, "Donna, Harriet, Barbara, Shirley, Marjorie, Jane, Florence." See if her tongue-in-cheek analysis doesn't strike at the truth:

> For two decades, during the Fifties and Sixties, they were the role models for every mother in the country. They looked better cleaning their houses than most of us looked at our weddings.
>
> They never lost their temper, gained weight, spent more money than their husbands made, or gave viewers any reason not to believe they were living their lives in celibacy. . . .
>
> It was the age of God, Motherhood, Flag, and Apple Pie. All you had to do to be a mother was to put on an apron.

No one did it better than these prime-time mothers. . . .

It was the not-ready-for-prime-time mothers who questioned it in the late Sixties.

They questioned the long days. The lack of fringe benefits. The run-and-fetch syndrome. The question "What kind of a day did you have?" and the answer that fell on deaf ears.

It started out as a ripple of discontent, gathering momentum through the Seventies. By the Eighties the dissidents were a force to be dealt with. . . .

Whatever happened to the Insulin Seven: Donna, Barbara, Shirley, Harriet, Marjorie, Jane, and Florence? They disappeared beneath a tidal wave of reality.[2]

Bombeck's comments here are right on target. In her inimitable style, she shows that the prime-time model of the All-American family was nothing but an image. It never really existed—except in Hollywood studios (and, today, in reruns). For a time it served as a pattern to which many of us aspired (and, according to Gallup, still do). But in the end, its unreality was crudely exposed by the vicious tongues of an unrestrained, expressive sixties generation.

Is "Traditional" the Same as "Biblical"?

Nevertheless, many in the Church today speak as if the traditional model is actually the biblical model of what a family ought to be. I can understand why. With divorce now epidemic, wife and child abuse at an all-time high, and violence skyrocketing among youth, who among us would not want the stability, the security, and frankly, the affluence that seems inherent in the traditional model? Nevertheless, I believe our desire to go back in time is misplaced.

What was the traditional family of the fifties and sixties really like? Frankly, it had flaws—major structural flaws. It looked pretty appealing on television. And countless households gave the appearance of living every bit as smoothly as the Cleavers. But in reality, they were pursuing a distortion of what God originally intended. Let me mention three problems that, sadly, went unnoticed.

ABSENTEE FATHERS

First, in the traditional family the father was conspicuously absent. Those of us who grew up in this era know this all too well. During the boom of postwar America, men overindulged in the promises, the opportunities, and the privileges that the times afforded in abundance. It became normal — expected, even — for a man to park his family in a suburb and indulge himself in the city earning a living.

This meant spending most of his waking hours away from home. But no one questioned that. Quite the opposite: It was the man who put in the longest hours who had the best chance of rising in the company and achieving status and power. Meanwhile, a man's family could hardly complain of his absence in light of all the wonderful things his expanding income enabled them to buy.

Here, then, was the All-American, traditional family, dedicated to the American Dream. But there was a dark side to the arrangement. The problem was not with the man's work itself.[3] The problem was that the father's absence created an irreplaceable void in the home. What's more, even when he was home in the evenings and on the weekends, he was unavailable. That is, *his* emotions and inner life were not open for his wife and children to see.

We are now discovering the devastating impact this physical and emotional detachment has wrought on American life, especially among men. Harvard psychologist Samuel Osherson calls it "one of the great underestimated tragedies of our times."[4] Citing an impressive body of research, he shows that the majority of men passing through mid-life today (i.e., male baby boomers) never experienced the presence of a father in a way that helped them learn what it means to be a healthy man. As a result, they are now pursuing a lifelong search to "find their fathers."

Finding our fathers. What a contrast to "Make Room for Daddy." A similar show produced today would have to be titled "Where Is Daddy?"[5] The traditional family permitted and even encouraged men to "love" their families by neglecting them in the interest of earning a living and achieving career success.

DEVALUED WOMEN

If the traditional family created headaches for fathers and, in turn, for their sons, it also *abandoned* and abused wives and daughters. A second flaw in the traditional concept of the home was that women were neither esteemed nor challenged.

United States technology, having so powerfully and decisively brought victory in World War II, was then channeled into domestic production. It provided the man with mobility through new cars and new superhighways on which to drive them. To the woman (at home) it advertised an endless catalog of "labor-saving" gadgets that were supposed to ease her housework and free up her time. But no one resolved the question: *Time for what?* The most common answer: Time for supporting her husband in his career and for raising children.

There is nothing wrong with saving time and energy. Nor is there any shame in helping one's husband and children become all that God intends them to be. But in the traditional family, the woman's value and identity were measured *only* with reference to husband and children. Who a woman was and what she was worth were defined in relation to *them,* never in terms of *herself* as an individual. She was never regarded as a person in her own right, with legitimate thoughts, desires, and ambitions. Indeed, the "unattached" woman — whether unmarried, divorced, or widowed — was regarded as an anomaly whose major goal ought to be to secure a husband.

The church could have spoken eloquently to this issue. But unfortunately it became a major advocate for the Donna Reed wife. It more or less endorsed the notion of the United States as a man's world, allowing Dad to frolic in the amenities that the times provided. Meanwhile, women felt increasingly unidentified as persons in their own right, unsupported, isolated, restless, and bored. In the end, they felt used. So when the turbulent forces of the sixties exploded, it was not surprising that women would be among the first to demand liberation from the traditional family.

MUTUAL TOLERANCE

There was a third problem with the traditional model: its misuse of the institution of marriage itself. Too often, the marriage became nothing more than a contract that kept two people together in a legal and financial partnership. That's a far cry from God's original intention, which calls two people to be fused together into "one flesh" intimacy. Sadly, even today many misuse the institution. They stand at the altar and recite beautiful vows, yet have little intention and even less practical understanding of how to share life together in any intimate way—emotionally, psychologically, or spiritually.

That kind of marriage is little more than a commitment to mutual tolerance. I know, because that was the case for my own parents, and maybe for your parents as well. A husband might drink too much, work too much, take on too many interests outside the home. He might nurse habits that his wife deplored. He might be too demanding or overly self-serving. Yet because of the marriage contract, the wife would say, "Well, I married him. I guess that's the way it has to be."

On the other hand, a wife might not take any interest in who her husband was or what he did, only in how much money he made and what she could buy with it. She might decline to participate in his interests or, worse, be highly critical of them. Perhaps she would lack empathy for the pressures he was under. Maybe she would be too religious. Yet because of the marriage contract, her husband would resign himself to the situation. "I'll never understand her," he'd sigh, "but I married her, so I guess I'll have to make the best of it."

A commitment to mutual tolerance. It was really a contract to "live together separately." Not that the two lives never touched; they seemed remarkably united when it came to pursuing the American Dream of a rising standard of living, home ownership, two cars in the garage, college educations for the children, and so on. But that did nothing to weld the couple together (except to make them mutually liable for debt). Many traditional marriages suffered a slow and agonizing death from what Sheldon Vanauken has termed "creeping separateness":

> The killer of love is creeping separateness. Inloveness is a gift of the gods, but then it is up to the lovers to cherish or to ruin.

Taking love for granted, especially after marriage. Ceasing to do things together. Finding separate interests. "We" turning into "I." Self. Self-regard: what *I* want to do. Actual selfishness only a hop away. This was the way of creeping separateness. And in the modern world, especially in the cities, everything favoured it. The man going off to his office; the woman staying home with the children—*her* children—or perhaps having a different job. The failure of love might seem to be caused by hate or boredom or unfaithfulness with a lover; but those were the results. First came the creeping separateness: the failure behind the failure.[6]

BUT WHAT'S THE ALTERNATIVE?

The tradition-spurning sixties generation refused to buy this marriage of mutual tolerance. Baby boomers came of age and began to ask, "Why should we do this to ourselves? If this is marriage, who needs it?" Sociologists, psychologists, even religious leaders had no immediate, compelling answer. They were dumbstruck by our generation's wholesale repudiation of our parents' arrangement. As I said, the church had a unique opportunity to respond to the growing social chaos. But it didn't. Now we need to start making up for lost time.

It won't be easy. After almost thirty-five years of alternatives to the traditional marriage, many boomers feel exhausted and hopeless about male/female relationships. Few seem interested in a return to the fifties. And while experiments like open marriages, communal living, trial marriages, and living together sounded appealing in the sixties and seventies, they now ring hollow. In fact, they've produced nothing short of a national tragedy. It makes me want to weep, especially for the children of those ugly experiments.

Today, young men and women in their twenties and thirties are afraid to give themselves to one another in any capacity. They want relationships yet they fear intimacy because they haven't seen much success in intimate relationships. They haven't seen much love, or concern, or permanence. They seem emotionally paralyzed, incapable of fully entrusting themselves to another person. Whenever I see this, I feel someone ought to apologize for the mess things are in. But no one wants to take responsibility. Those who once advocated all the new alternatives are long gone.

The United States has rightly rejected the traditional family as it really existed. Yet nothing better has replaced it. That's why I believe God's people have a wonderful opportunity at this moment in history. We do have an alternative to offer, one that will meet our hearts' desire for love, trust, fairness, and mutual fulfillment. But to seize the moment, we must separate ourselves from the "marriage that never was," the so-called traditional family. We need to admit its flaws and then shout from the rooftops that it was never God's design in the first place.

5
Searching for the Biblical Ideal

In any marriage, roles are important—make that *critically* important! If you want your marriage to succeed, you have to feel complete confidence and clarity about who does what and why. Without such understanding, you'll never feel satisfied.

Remember Debbie and John in chapter 1? Like many modern couples, they started out by de-emphasizing roles; they wanted to achieve equality in their relationship. But as Debbie discovered—along with countless others—there are no roleless marriages.

Without question, the very idea of roles is negative for some people today, especially for some women. They see roles as confining. Roles put people in a box. Roles limit choices. Roles keep women "in their place." Any talk of roles brings ugly images of abuse that women have had to endure. The whole notion of roles has become suspect as a backward, chauvinistic way of looking at relationships.

Well, that's not what I mean by roles. In this book, when I speak of a role, I mean *the essential function* that God has designed a man or a woman to fulfill in a marriage relationship. Let me add that while those roles differ, that does not mean that one is superior and one is inferior. Both are of equal value and importance. Hear me well on this point: As far as Scripture is concerned, roles address one's responsibility, not one's rank.

SYMBIOSIS

Think back to whatever biology you studied in school. You may recall that some organisms exist in what scientists call a *symbiotic relationship*. That is, two different species live side by side and perform certain functions that are indispensable to the life and well being of each other.

For instance, my sons and I once watched a television program in which a species of large fish suffered from parasites in its gills. In time these pesky invaders would injure the fish, even causing it to die. Fortunately, the larger fish had teamed up with a buddy—a much smaller fish that thrived on those parasites. This fish was small enough that it could actually swim into the open jaws and through the gills of its "friend," enjoying a parasite meal as it went.

In exchange for this "pest control," the large fish kept away hungry predators that would otherwise have enjoyed a tasty dinner of the little worker. These two fish lived in a symbiotic relationship in which both species fulfilled vital, complementary roles.

Obviously, any notion of superiority/inferiority was irrelevant. What was relevant was life and its quality. Each fish brought about a better life for the other.

God created man and woman to live in such a symbiotic relationship in marriage—not to have the same functions, but to have *complementary* functions. Each partner must play his or her God-given role. Those roles have to do with responsibility, not rank. And they have everything to do with the quality of life the couple will enjoy.

So far I have tried to distinguish the biblical pattern of marriage from "traditional" and "egalitarian" forms without explaining the differences. These differences are sometimes subtle and sometimes striking, but always important. At some points the traditional view sounds like the biblical view; at other points the egalitarian arrangement sounds biblical. Don't be misled! Similarities exist only because these two views have borrowed heavily from the biblical model. Unfortunately, they take certain selected parts to extremes that I believe are imbalanced and hurtful.

By contrast, a biblical marriage is a perfect blend of structure and equality, offering balance and beauty. It is that blend so many couples desperately seek today—most without even realizing it. Sadly, they will never find it in these less-than-biblical extremes.

THE HUSBAND'S ROLE

In a biblical marriage, the husband's role revolves around "leadership." Now if you hold to a more egalitarian position, you may react and cry "foul"! You may jump to the conclusion that I'm just another chauvinist advocating the oppression of women through a hierarchical model of male dominance. Nothing could be further from the truth.

Biblical leadership is anything but that. Instead, it follows the pattern Jesus set forth in Luke 22:24-26:

> There arose also a dispute among them as to which one of them was regarded to be greatest. And He said to them, "The kings of the Gentiles lord it over them; and those who have

authority over them are called 'Benefactors.' But not so with you, but let him who is the greatest among you become as the youngest, and the leader as the servant."

Wives, are you afraid that if your husband is the "leader," he'll dominate you? That's what Jesus is addressing here. Force and domination always have been common bedfellows with most leadership styles. Leaders too often "lord it over" other people. They become "benefactors," the ones who get all the benefits of the relationship at the expense of everyone else. If you're afraid of that, I don't blame you. Too many homes, including Christian ones, have degenerated into this style of leadership. Women have suffered untold hurt and humiliation as a result.

Servant
Leader

But that kind of leadership totally contradicts biblical teaching. Notice again Jesus' stern rebuke that follows this description of abusive power: "But not so with you"! The kind of leadership Jesus defines for His followers has to do with:

- *Responsibility*, not privilege.
- *Service*, not being served.
- *Support*, not superiority.

By the way, that's the same kind of leadership style Paul had in mind when he said that the husband is the "head" of the wife (Ephesians 5:23). We'll talk more about that in part 2, when we look at the husband's role in greater detail.

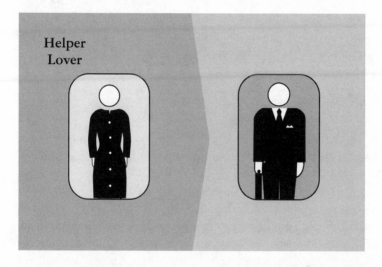

Helper
Lover

THE WIFE'S ROLE

What about the wife? What is her role in the marriage? Time and again Christian books present the wife's role in terms of "submission." That's the common view. But it is a major mistake! Not only is it a misreading of Scripture, but it is one of the chief reasons why so many women spurn what they mistakenly take to be the biblical model of marriage. I can't imagine anything that lowers a woman's expectations of marriage more than to tell her, "Your role is to submit." Think about it: What that really means is that she should do nothing! Just get out of the way! What kind of role is that?!

It's not that submission has no place in a marriage. It does. It's a biblical term. But unfortunately, submission has been misused and misinterpreted, as we'll see in chapter 17. If we want to understand the wife's role wholistically, we have to look beyond the few statements on submission to the many statements that portray her as an active, creative, dynamic, and contributing member of the marriage.[1]

When we do this, we find that God calls a wife to a positive, creative, challenging, and vital role in the family. Her role revolves around helping and loving. Without these contributions, her husband and children will be at great loss. She offers them a one-of-a-kind support and nurturing that no one else can provide. If she callously ignores or abandons this function, her family will be destabilized and damaged in catastrophic ways. As Proverbs 14:1 says:

> The wise woman builds her house,
> But the foolish tears it down with her own hands.

The biblical role for a wife is the way of wisdom. It is not something she should view as optional, but as a nonnegotiable.

RUNNING FROM THE ROLES

Keep in mind what I said earlier about a symbiotic relationship. Leading and nurturing are very different responsibilities, demanding very different approaches and mindsets. It's almost impossible to do them both at the same time, as any single parent can tell you. In fact, we get a hint of just how different they are by noting that God created two different genders, male and female, to fulfill them. The two functions are that unique. By design, both are critical to the success of a family. Neither sex could handle everything alone, thus the need for symbiosis in the marriage relationship.

Yet it's fair to say that in most marriages today, even among Christians, husbands are not leading, and in turn, wives are not nurturing in ways advocated by Scripture. Sure, men are still "in control" in many marriages. But despite what they may think, these men are not leading—more likely they're exploiting! I don't blame women for condemning that behavior.

Some women simply don't know how to nurture. It's an art that they've never seen. Having children scares them. Many young, professional women especially feel ambivalent about starting a family. Tending to a home and kids seems foreign and alien, maybe even repulsive.

At the same time, many wives have buried their instincts of nurturing. Many have had to in order to protect themselves and their children. They don't want to depend on exploitative males who use them, abuse them, and abandon them. Thus when we look today at relationships between the sexes, we see that fear is increasing and intimacy is decreasing.

Frankly, I see no reversal of these trends until men begin to lead as God intended. When they do, women will feel the freedom to do what is instinctive within them, and that is to nurture.

How This Book Can Help Your Marriage

As we launch into the heart of this book, let me assure you of my deep concern for your marriage. Rather than providing one more "expert" opinion that will change with next year's fashion, I want to help you discover timeless principles from the Bible about how God designed and organized marriage, and how those principles can affect your relationship. Based on the feedback I've received from hundreds of couples who've interacted with this same material, you can expect a number of significant benefits, including:

- *Clarity on what the Bible teaches about roles.* It's time to start thinking differently about roles! It's also time to redefine submission, *and* introduce its masculine counterpart. We'll do that in part 6.
- *A wholistic concept of marital roles.* I'm going to introduce an idea called "core roles." You'll discover that biblical roles do not encompass everything in marriage, only some things. But they do provide essential structure and direction. I'll also introduce some "core concerns" that husbands and wives ought to have for one another. These concerns are the keys to marriage satisfaction.
- *Hope for wives.* Do you feel confused, hurt, and angry as a wife? Maybe you've heard too many mixed messages— and seen too few positive results. If so, you'll be eager to learn that you *can* fulfill your roles as a woman, a wife, a mother, a worker—and still please God. You don't have to fear God's "role call" for you; there's liberty in it!

- *Hope for husbands*. With all the discussion about women's rights in the past two decades, many of us men feel "bashed" and misunderstood. Our insecurities and inadequacies have been laid bare, but not laid to rest. This book can help by articulating our feelings and addressing our concerns. As a man, I also think you'll appreciate the "big picture" of marriage that is offered.
- *Practical help in applying biblical principles to your marriage*. The ultimate test of this book is its *usefulness* to you and your spouse. Many couples have taken the principles and strategies presented here and used them to transform their relationships. I can't answer every question or solve every problem, but I promise an approach to marriage that is realistic, practical, and biblical.

ACCEPT NO SUBSTITUTES!

I grew up on Cornflakes. But lately, a host of exotic cereals have moved Cornflakes to the back of the grocer's shelf and on to hard times. So Kellogg came up with a variety of spots in which an actor shovels a heaping spoonful of crunchy flakes into his mouth as a narrator says, "Cornflakes — taste them again for the first time." What a catchy and appealing line! It tells us we've forgotten how wonderful this original cereal was. And it calls us to return and experience it again.

What happened to Cornflakes is similar to what has happened to the Bible's model for marriage. If we ever did know it, we've abandoned it for a host of exotic substitutes, some of which claim to be "new and improved." But these "new" models — including the "traditional" arrangement — are nothing but cheap substitutes. We need to get back to the original, authentic, biblical model and "taste it again for the first time." When we do, I think we'll discover the beauty and the power that was there all along. Let's begin, shall we?

FOR DISCUSSION

1. Many couples try to base their roleless marriages on good qualities—even biblical ones—such as fairness, justice, and respect. How would you relate these positive qualities to your marriage? Are there areas in your marriage where you believe these qualities are lacking? Explain.

2. Read Luke 22:24-27. While they're not specifically about marriage, these verses describe the role of a servant-leader. Jesus exemplified this role. In your own words, define servant-leader. What qualities does he possess? Husbands, do you see those qualities in yourself? Wives, do you see these qualities in your husband?

3. Read Proverbs 14:1. This verse says a "wise woman builds her house." Do you agree that wives are called to be nurturers—lovers of their husbands and children? What are the qualities of a nurturer? Wives, do you see these qualities in yourself? Husbands, do you see these qualities in your wife?

4. Which kind of marriage would you say your marriage most closely resembles at present? The traditional marriage? The qulitarian marriage? or The biblical marriage? Would your spouse agree or disagree with your assessment?

5. What marriage insight in Part I impacted you the most? Share it with your spouse and tell them why it was so meaningful to you.

Close this time of discussion in prayer. Ask God to help you each to understand your role in your marriage, to better fulfill those roles, and to supply His strength to live up to the responsibility He created for you in your marriage.

Part Two

THE HUSBAND'S CORE ROLE

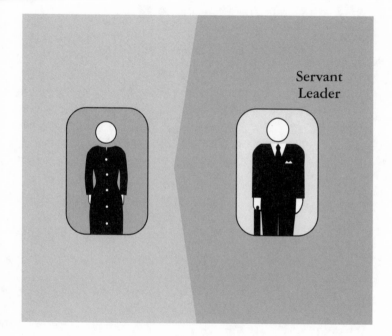

Servant
Leader

6

The High Calling
of Headship

Several years ago, while waiting at Atlanta's Harttsfield airport for
a flight home to Little Rock, I happened on an interesting article in
the *Atlanta Journal.* A bold headline pronounced: "New Swiss
Marriage Law Ends Men's Reign as Head of House."

"On January 1, husbands lost their position as undisputed
head of the family," the article began. It went on to explain that for
nearly a century, Swiss law had precisely defined the roles of the
sexes. Men had complete power to dispose of assets and assume
debts, to decide where their families would live and how their children would be educated. There was even a provision requiring a
wife who wanted employment to secure her husband's permission
first. But a new Swiss law had toppled men from their traditional
household thrones. Under the new legal arrangement, according to
the article:

- The roles of men and women in marriage will now be left
  undefined. Husbands and wives will determine for themselves how professional and domestic tasks are to be shared.
- A woman may retain her maiden name upon marriage.
- Husbands and wives are responsible only for their personal
  debts.

- The wife retains control of her own finances and property.
- The wife can now have access to her husband's tax files.[1]

In a country as conservative and steeped in tradition as Switzerland, this law has predictably encountered great resistance—especially among husbands! Nevertheless, a new social order has arrived, with sweeping implications. Headship has been voted out. And not just in Switzerland, but everywhere!

Amid this massive social change, any affirmation of headship sounds backward, discriminatory, anti-women. Anyone who promotes it becomes an easy target for criticism, slander, even revenge! A vote for headship is equated with a vote for oppression of females. On the other hand, a vote for equality is a vote for women's liberation. So, how do you vote?

Personally, I refuse to accept this kind of either/or polarity so popular today. As a Christian, I vote for *both*. I'm for headship *and* for woman's equality. I don't see that as inconsistent or a copout. There is a delicate balance in my vote, which the rest of this book explains. In this chapter, let's begin with the sticky subject of headship. What are the issues and what does the Bible say?

HEADSHIP: A RADICALLY NEW APPROACH

Ephesians 5 defines headship as clearly and forcefully as any passage of Scripture. It says (verses 23-30, NIV; emphasis added):

> For the husband is the *head* of the wife as Christ is the *head* of the church, his body, of which he is the Savior. Now as the church submits to Christ, so also wives should submit to their husbands in everything.
>
> Husbands, love your wives, just as Christ loved the church and gave himself up for her to make her holy, cleansing her by the washing with water through the word, and to present her to himself as a radiant church, without stain or wrinkle or any other blemish, but holy and blameless. In this same way, husbands ought to love their wives as their own bodies. He who loves his wife loves himself. After all, no one ever hated his

own body, but he feeds and cares for it, just as Christ does the church—for we are members of his body.

This passage is not hard to understand, is it? Not really. It may be hard to swallow by today's standards, or hard to work out in real life. But it's not hard to understand. It says that the husband is responsible for leadership in the home. He is called the "head."

Unfortunately, some Christians dismiss this term by saying that Paul is merely restating a view of marriage that was common in the ancient world. According to that view, a man was the absolute master of his family, and his wife and children were under his complete and total dominion. Paul supposedly held to that view early in his ministry but changed it later. As a result, Ephesians 5 does not express the will of God for marriage, but rather a cultural norm to which Paul temporarily subscribed, they say.

But that makes no sense. Why would Paul need to command wives to yield to the leadership of their husbands if they were already doing so? Likewise, why would he challenge husbands to lead in a specific way if, in fact, they were already doing that? Why reinforce what was common practice? That was never Paul's style. The truth is, it was *not* common practice. On the contrary, family life in the Roman Empire was in shambles at the time Paul penned these words. Divorce and adultery were running rampant. Amid the fantastic wealth that Rome enjoyed, the marriage bond was suffering a complete and utter breakdown. Many couples were embracing lifestyles of independence with little, if any, commitment to one another. Women were spurning the home and traditional ultra-authoritarian concepts of male leadership that had been practiced during the beginning days of the Empire.

In Ephesus, Paul's words connecting male headship to God and Christ must have sounded ludicrous, because the Ephesians worshiped a *female* deity! A city of 300,000, Ephesus enjoyed a major tourist economy thanks to its Temple of Artemis, one of the Seven Wonders of the World. Artemis, or Diana as the Romans called her, was the goddess of virginity, among other things. The shrine at Ephesus housed a multi-breasted image that supposedly had fallen out of the sky.

Paul had caused a full-scale riot there with his new and strange teaching (Acts 19:23-41). So his words advocating a special kind of male headship, rather than simply restating an existing cultural norm, probably offended many of those who read or heard them.

The situation was no different at Corinth. Sophisticated and extraordinarily wealthy, the Corinthians struggled when it came to issues of men and women. Men didn't want to be leaders, and women didn't want to be led. In fact, they didn't even want to talk about the issue. Yet Paul told them the same thing he told the Ephesians:

> I want you to understand that Christ is the head of every man, and the man is the head of a woman, and God is the head of Christ. (1 Corinthians 11:3)

Rather than caving in to the egalitarian drift of his culture or trying to revive ancient patterns of male authoritarianism, Paul spoke distinctively and courageously to the issue of male and female roles in marriage. Under the inspiration of the Holy Spirit, he designated a "core role" of leadership for the man and described it in terms of Christ's leadership of His church. This was something unheard of. It was strange, unique, and for a society going in the opposite direction, scary.

WHAT DOES "HEAD" MEAN?

That brings us to the word *head* itself. What does *head* mean? This is an extremely important question because there has been a great deal of misunderstanding as well as misinformation on this subject.

Perhaps you've discovered how the meaning of words can change over time. My little boy plays with some special toy cars during his bath. These cars are coated with a heat-sensitive material. When placed in water, they slowly change colors, much to his delight. His red car magically transforms into a yellow one.

Words can be like that as they are "bathed" in different time periods. Their meanings can slowly change colors. We've witnessed a few such transformations in our own day. Take the word *cool,* for instance. Though still used to describe a range of temperature, it has also taken on the meaning of describing the appeal of someone or something. *Gay* once meant happy. Today, we rarely think of that meaning when we hear it. Words change meanings!

It's not surprising, then, to discover that the word *head* has changed colors as well over the last two thousand years. Sometimes I ask people, "What does the word *head* bring to mind in the context of marriage?" Most often the responses I receive have to do with an "authoritarian" hue: "boss," "ruler," "superior rank," "owner," "president," "executive," "dictator." These terms usually have strong emotions attached to them.

But if we were to ask that same "head" question to the early Christians who first understood Paul's radical usage of the term, I believe we would receive responses with a much different, "life-giving" color: "protector," "provider," "lover," "responsible for," "developer of." Read through Ephesians 5 again and see for yourself whether this "life-giving" tint is not clearly evident.

Of course, one meaning has remained constant throughout the ages, whenever the word *head* has been applied symbolically to a person. It always implies *leadership*. Whether it's "head of the class," "head of the army," or "head of the home," to be a "head" means to be a leader. It meant that in Paul's day, and it continues to mean that now. Any attempt to extract the thought of leadership from the word *head* ranges from poor scholarship to outright deception.[2] So at issue is not whether a "head" is a leader. The issue is this: *What kind of leader?*

Paul had a radically different kind of leadership in mind than his first-century contemporaries. It was revolutionary. Unheard of! By drawing from the life of Jesus, Paul forever altered our understanding of leadership in marriage. You see, Paul colored male headship with:

- Responsibility, not rank.
- Sacrifice, not selfishness.
- Duty, not domination.

Men, *your* role as a husband is to lead in these Christlike colors. You are to seek your wife's best, even at your own expense.

Headship defined this way becomes a high and holy calling.

Are you challenged by that? I think Paul's male readers were. When they read (or heard) Ephesians 5, I think they were deeply touched and remarked, "What an incredible calling!"

I remember reading one of Gary Larson's "Far Side" cartoons showing Robin Hood on bended knee, handing a bag full of money to two surprised porcupines. The caption read: "Historic note: Until his life's destiny was further clarified, Robin Hood spent several years robbing from the rich and giving to the porcupines."[3]

In the same way, the destiny of a marriage greatly depends on role clarity. Until you as a husband understand what being a "head" really involves, you'll be just as lost and off-target as poor Robin Hood. Headship is a calling to empower another human being; it's not a license to indulge yourself. It's an historic moment when a man finally embraces the meaning of that radical distinction.

HEADSHIP UNDER THE CURSE

Some people may ask, "Doesn't it say in Genesis 3 that a man is supposed to rule over his wife?" Not exactly. Here is the actual text of Genesis 3:16:

> To the woman He [God] said, ". . . your desire shall be for your husband, and he shall rule over you."

The Hebrew word translated "rule" means to dominate, to keep beneath, to rule over as an absolute sovereign. The word is used of kings and public officials throughout the Old Testament. But keep in mind that Genesis 3:16 is a statement of the curse, not of the kingdom. It foretells how *fallen* men will naturally tend to live with their wives. It prophesies that they will dominate them and subjugate them to positions of lower status. As we know, this has indeed been the case. We have thousands of cultures and thousands of years to document that this is exactly what has happened. Women have struggled under the harsh dominance of natural men for centuries. Even today, the mournful wails that proceed from too many homes come as a result of the rule of selfish and insensitive bullies.

HEADSHIP UNDER CHRIST

Harsh dominance is not the way of Christ. So, when Paul says that a man is the head of his wife as Christ is the head of the church, he's not supporting the curse—he's breaking it! He's showing how we men can break the cycle of misery and the "me-first" mentality that the Fall inaugurated.

But for that to happen, we first must commit ourselves to Jesus' leadership style, as outlined in Luke 22, a passage we looked at in the last chapter. Speaking to his disciples, Jesus said (verse 25),

> "The kings of the Gentiles lord it over them; and those who have authority over them are called 'Benefactors.'"

A "benefactor" is one who receives the benefits. In the ancient world, many rulers used force and employed their supreme power to enrich themselves at the expense of helpless people. In our own day, the lifting of the veil on communism has shown many modern scenes of similar abuses. Likewise, there are many, many homes today in which husbands "lord it over" their wives and children, receiving all the benefits, all the perks, all the advantages. Meanwhile, the women and kids come up short.

That's why Jesus says (verses 26-27),

> "But not so with you, but let him who is greatest among you become as the youngest, and the leader as the servant. For who is greater, the one who reclines at the table, or the one who serves? Is it not the one who reclines at the table?"

We are tempted to say "yes" to this question. That's how we naturally think. It's also our world's view. However, Jesus is not talking about what is natural or popular, but about what is supernatural. That's why verse 27 ends with Him saying,

> "But I am among you as one who serves."

Matthew records the same incident (20:28):

"The Son of Man did not come to be served, but to serve."

Servant and leader are not terms that are naturally congruous. They seem to contradict one another. Yet, in God's Kingdom, to be the "head" is to be this unique blend of leader and servant. It's true, men, that you and I have been given the authority to lead our wives; but our style is to be that of a servant, not a lord. Our aim is not to suck the life out of our wives, but to be a source of life to them. Only then can we claim the title "head" as God proclaimed it in Christ.

I make it a practice in each wedding ceremony I perform to challenge the groom with that kind of leadership. I warn him not to make the all-too-common mistake of assuming "headship" means special privileges or ultimate power. "Remember," I say, "your leadership is to be modeled after Christ's leadership of His bride, the Church. Christ didn't use the Church. He didn't dominate her, or force His leadership on her. On the contrary, He *earned* the right of leadership by expending Himself for His bride, and ultimately by dying for her. It was a cross that gave Jesus the ultimate right to lead."

Then I say,

In the same way, you must *earn* the right to be the head of your home. And yet, you can do that only when there is a similar cross in your own life. Only as you die to your own selfishness, only as you willingly give yourself up for your bride—only then can you begin to be a Christlike "head." The daily sting of your "death to self" must always be the starting point of your leadership. Christ calls you to lead and also to die! This is servant-leadership.

Sobering, isn't it? Biblical leadership is clearly not a place of ease and advantage, but a calling to work, sacrifice, and service. Anything less than that kind of headship deserves to be voted out!

7

Lording Leader
or Serving Leader?

Sherard and I were enjoying a meal with another couple once when the woman asked me, "If the ideal husband, the ideal wife, the Easter Bunny, and Santa Claus were all standing on a street corner together, who would cross the street first?"

It was an obvious setup with a twist I knew I would enjoy. So I said, "I don't know. Which one?"

"The ideal wife would cross first," she laughed. "All the rest are figments of your imagination!"

Although we all laughed, there was a sense of reality behind her story. Does an ideal husband exist? Is he out there? What does he look like? Today, with so much change in regard to marriage, I think you'd be hard pressed to get any consistent answer. On top of that, there's a growing cynicism among women about men altogether, and much less trust.

In the last chapter, I tried to paint a portrait of the ideal (not perfect) husband. Granted, it was mostly theoretical and wrapped in theological terms, but nevertheless it serves as a starting point. It gives us a helpful vocabulary to draw from. "Servant-leader" becomes the reference point from which to measure any ideal husbanding. It also serves as a title of honor that men can pursue. We men need this title to challenge us! We also need it to know what

marital role we're to strive for. "Servant-leader" sums it up suc-
cinctly and accurately. Personally, it's been the North Star that has
kept me on course throughout my married life. There's no better
question to ask myself from time to time than this: "Have I been
acting like a servant-leader recently?" There's also no greater
compliment than to be called "servant-leader" by my wife.

But let's get more specific, more practical. Just what does a
"servant-leader" look like in the everyday, ordinary situations of
married life? In this chapter, I want to present six practical
descriptions of the servant-leader. In doing so, I'll show how he
handles six issues common to every marriage. His approach con-
trasts sharply with the authoritarian, "lording" leader that Jesus
referred to in Luke 22. Let me show you the difference.

PRACTICAL ISSUES

Decision Making

The lording leader loves to give orders. He's the boss. He has to
have control. He makes all the decisions; everyone else just carries
out his directives. If anyone questions his decisions, he silences
them with another string of commands. That's because he's not
interested in questions, suggestions, or better ideas. He's only interested in action, in getting things done *his* way.

There's absolutely no flexibility with the lording leader, even when
it's obvious he's wrong. "Let's eat Mexican food tonight," he says.

"The kids and I had Mexican food for lunch," his wife replies.
"What about that new Italian restaurant?"

"We're going out for Mexican food!" he insists. "And that's
that!"

Discussion always is a threat to the lording leader. When he
works in the yard with his son, he doesn't ask whether the boy
wants to edge or mow. He just declares, "You can mow. Edging is
my job!" End of discussion.

By contrast, the servant-leader seeks to hear what others in the
family think. He stays open to better alternatives, even if they're
not his. He's willing to listen. It's not that he never takes the initiative; in fact, he often does. But in setting direction for the family,

he takes the needs and concerns of each member into account, and considers how the choices will affect each one. His chief concern is to do what is *best* for everyone involved. This isn't easy; it takes time and a measure of diplomacy. But it builds a healthy sense of teamwork into the family.

So, when the servant-leader's wife says, "Honey, I'm tired. Can we eat out tonight?" he might check his wallet and say, "We can't afford anything expensive. But yeah, let's go get a pizza. You need a break!" In the yard he listens when his son asks, "Dad, can I edge?" He learns that this is a teachable moment, not a threat.

Understanding a Wife's Needs

The lording leader knows little about women. He ignores his wife's distinctively feminine needs. To be honest, he's never really given them much thought. He's never done any research on them, that's for sure. He treats his wife pretty much on the basis of stereotypes that come from unholy quarters.

For instance, the lording leader can't stand it when his wife cries. If they get into an argument, she holds her own for a while, but sooner or later she breaks down in tears. He can feel it coming. And when she does he always says, "There you go. Just like a woman!" He doesn't respect her feelings. They make no sense to him.

It's not that way with the servant-leader. He lives with his wife "in an understanding way," as 1 Peter 3:7 puts it. He responds to her sensitively, out of a wealth of knowledge about her needs and concerns. He accepts that she is different from him, and doesn't patronize her or demean her because she is a woman.

In fact, the servant-leader reads widely to understand her world. He even asks her to recommend books and articles that will give him insight into her perspective. And he listens when she talks about herself. Over time, his growing understanding of his wife unleashes all kinds of new communication and intimacy into their marriage.

Conflict

The lording leader becomes defensive when his wife challenges him with her own thoughts and views. He views everything from a win/lose perspective. He can't stand to be wrong and let his wife be right. He certainly can't admit to her when he's wrong. So he browbeats her into going along with him, and manipulates her into granting his wishes.

One time a lording leader loaned money to a certain friend. His wife warned him that she didn't trust the man. "What do you know?!" he told her. "I've been around this guy since college. Besides, he's a lot more reliable than that stupid brother of yours!" After a barrage of statements like these, she realized it was no use trying to make him see her perspective and gave up. Later, when the fellow left town without repaying the loan, she had the good sense to bite her tongue. Her husband never did get paid back. Of course, the outcome wasn't important to her husband. He cared only about "winning" the discussion.

By contrast, the servant-leader is interested in arriving at the truth, in knowing what is right, not in who is "winning." He's a man of truth, not a scorekeeper. And he knows that his wife brings a valuable perspective and sensitivity to many issues that he barely understands. So he values her input, and together they determine what is right.

When one servant-leader wanted to refurbish the garage, his wife said, "Are you sure? We're going to move in a couple of years, and I don't feel we should waste our money on that project." So instead of proceeding, he sat down with his wife to talk about their needs, their plans, and their finances. Eventually they worked out a compromise.

Strengths and Weaknesses
The lording leader loves to point out the flaws and failures of his wife. He stays busy doing so, especially when her deficiencies prevent him from enjoying the benefits he feels he's entitled to. Day and night he tears her down, as if by criticism he could make her a better person.

For instance, the lording leader always has a criticism to offer about his wife's housework and cooking. He calls it teasing, but he doesn't notice that she never smiles when he does it. One time she knocked herself out to prepare a meal for his boss. When everyone sat down to eat, the guests complimented her on the entree. Finally her husband said, "If only she could cook this well every night!"

By contrast, the servant-leader majors on what's right and good about his wife. Yes, he's aware of her weaknesses. But his focus is on her strengths and assets. He constantly affirms her, emphasizing her significance and importance to his life. He knows that encouragement gives her energy to grow and develop.

Every day before the servant-leader leaves for work he pauses to give her a giant hug. "You're the best!" he tells her, and plants an unhurried kiss on her lips.

Power

The lording leader pushes and manipulates his wife. He may even physically intimidate her to get his way. Because he doesn't want to face his own weaknesses and insecurities, he tries to reassure himself that he's "a real man" by asserting his power and masculinity in domineering, even violent ways.

A good example is the time the lording leader slapped his wife during an argument about the children. At one point she had accused him of being way too strict on the kids. When he denied it she cried, "Liar!" and in the heat of the moment he slapped her. Later he apologized, but she never forgot.

The servant-leader knows that he and his marriage would be the real losers if he ever resorted to physical intimidation. Regardless of whatever differences he might have with his wife, he has set his heart to value what she thinks is best for the marriage. Though it's never easy, he involves her in decisions and works hard to reach mutual agreement. His goal is to empower his wife to do what she needs to do, not assert his power in order to get his own way.

For instance, one Christmas the servant-leader's wife wanted to volunteer for a community service project. It meant several evenings away from home during December. It was a reasonable request, so he didn't complain. He knew it was important to her. He scheduled his time in order to make sure he'd be home with the kids on the nights she was out. And when the project was over, he helped her celebrate her participation.

Household Chores

A lording leader comes home and excuses himself from responsibility. In fact, he comforts himself with the thought that he *deserves* to be treated like royalty in light of all the abuse he has to put up with out in the work world. His wife is made to feel like hired help.

The lording leader doesn't do dishes. He doesn't pick up laundry. He doesn't cook, clean, or take out the trash. When he is forced into action, he makes sure everyone knows it's a real sacrifice, and not something he should be expected to do.

The servant-leader, on the other hand, pro-actively *manages* his home. He doesn't just pay attention to chores; he watches out for the pace of the home—his own pace as well as the pace of his wife and kids. He guards against a schedule that would brutalize them, especially his wife.

The servant-leader also sets the spiritual tone in the home. He tries to keep God's perspective in view and helps his family reflect biblically on things that happen in their lives. He also keeps his home a fun place, with a lot of smiles and laughter and celebration.

WHAT KIND OF LEADER ARE YOU?

No man matches completely the caricatures I've drawn. But men, if each of us is honest, we probably feel a strong pull to one side more than the other in each of the categories mentioned. So, what kind of leader are you in each category? Do some of the descriptions of the lording leader have an all-too-comfortable (or uncomfortable) fit? Would you like to do better? Does the idea of being a servant-leader inspire you?

These are questions I have to constantly ask myself. Various situations continually challenge me to choose which kind of leader I'm going to be. Recently, for example, my family was faced with the decision of purchasing a new van. The van we were driving had faithfully served our family for eleven years, but now it was in obvious pain.

In leading my family through the decision to buy a replacement, I realized that I could go about it in two different ways. On the one hand, I could just go out and make the decision myself. I could select the vehicle I wanted so that it reflected the image I desired. I could also do it impulsively, strapping our cash in such a way that the other areas of our household budget would suffer. In other words, I could make the decision as a "lording" leader.

On the other hand, I could be a servant-leader. I could work for mutual agreement. I could make sure that everybody in the family found something in the vehicle to get excited about, even if they had to give up something else. I could ask, "What sort of van works best for everyone involved?"

To be honest, that was a difficult process for me. To lead like that works against my natural state. But I had to remember that God isn't interested in developing my natural state; He wants to develop my supernatural state! He knows that in a good marriage things must benefit everyone in the family. And He wants me to reach high for that ideal, no matter how difficult it is. In fact, He wants me to die for that ideal. Remember, the husband's call is to lead and to die to self.

No One Said It Would Be Easy

I once heard about a young man who decided to be a servant-leader for his wife. So one day he gave her a "day off." He took their three-year-old son and, as part of his chores, went shopping for the family at the grocery store. Up and down the aisles they went, his little one in the cart. But it was getting toward the youngster's naptime, and he grew restless and cranky, and began to throw a fit. He screamed and yelled and reached out to grab things off the shelves, knocking over jars, cans, and boxes.

An older lady was walking behind the father, keen to observe how he was going to handle the weary rapscallion. She was amazed that the father stayed fairly calm. Every once in a while she heard him say things like, "Now, Ronnie, calm down." "Ronnie, don't do that! Don't get out of control." "Calm yourself, Ronnie. It's going to be all right." "Don't do that, Ronnie! If you do, someone's going to get hurt!" "Just a little longer, Ronnie! Hang in there, buddy."

On and on the monologue went, even as the child's tantrums grew worse. Finally, father and son arrived at the checkout counter, just in front of the lady. Standing in line, she tapped him on the shoulder and said with a smile, "You know, I just want to tell you, I've been watching you. I can see this has been a difficult situation. I just want to tell you how much I appreciate the way you handled little Ronnie."

At that the father's eyes grew big and he shook his head. Finally he said, "Ma'am, *I'm* Ronnie!"

We've all been there, haven't we? Ronnie shows us the reality of what it takes to be a servant-leader. He had to talk himself into dying. Men, in order to be servant-leaders, so must we. Ronnie had to continually remind himself that what he was doing was the best thing for his family because, at times, it didn't always feel like the best thing. To be a servant-leader, so must we. Yes, it's tough being a servant-leader. But it's also something else, something very special—it's right!

8

Twenty-Five Ways to Be a Servant-Leader

The term servant-leader has a solid ring to it, doesn't it? It sounds right. Few object to it. It makes sense not only to husbands but to wives as well.

Nevertheless, it's a term that needs practical handles attached to it. Otherwise, it will be a nice thought that never translates into real life. Whenever I present the concept of servant-leader, men express a real hunger for applications and practical pictures. What does this leadership model look like? Let me suggest twenty-five ways you can be a real-life servant-leader.

1. *A servant-leader includes his wife in envisioning the future.* He initiates periodic getaways with his wife, to dream together about where their marriage is headed. These "big picture" moments shape their direction and decision making. "Are we biting off too much?" "Are we both excited about where we're headed?" "What do we need to change?"

2. *A servant-leader accepts spiritual responsibility for his family.* For example, he accepts responsibility for how regularly they attend church, for praying at meals and at other times, for initiating discussion of spiritual issues among the family, and for making sure that all decisions harmonize with biblical principles.

3. *A servant-leader is willing to say "I'm sorry" and "forgive me" to his family.* He is able to admit when he's wrong.

4. *A servant-leader discusses household responsibilities with his wife and makes sure these are fairly distributed.* He also periodically readdresses this division of labor as the family changes.

5. *A servant-leader seeks the consultation of his wife on all major financial decisions.* He values her input and her agreement in these ventures.

6. *A servant-leader follows through with commitments he has made to his wife.* He honors her by this demonstration of integrity.

7. *A servant-leader anticipates the different stages his marriage will pass through (see chapter 25).* He reads about these upcoming stages and discusses them with others so he'll be ready to meet the unique pressures and challenges each one brings.

8. *A servant-leader, likewise, anticipates the stages his children will pass through.* He works with his wife to make the necessary changes that will keep their parenting relevant and effective in their children's emerging lives.

9. *A servant-leader frequently tells his wife what he likes about her.* He is *specific* about what makes her so special to him.

10. *A servant-leader provides financially for his family's basic living expenses.* He seeks to keep their lifestyle within *his* means in order to give flexibility to his wife.

11. *A servant-leader deals with distractions so that he can talk with his wife and family.* He turns off the television or puts down the newspaper. He wants to understand what is going on in their lives and in their feelings, and he doesn't want needless distractions to interrupt their conversations. They are important people!

12. *A servant-leader prays with his wife on a regular basis.* Besides being pleasing to God, this form of communication inspires a special intimacy between them.

13. *A servant-leader initiates meaningful family traditions,* such as these:

- Praying together as a family before special events and trips.
- Celebrating when his children pass the milestones of life—graduations, adulthood, leaving home, marriage, birth of grandchildren, and so on.

- Honoring his wife before his children on their wedding anniversary.
- Reading books to his children.
- Praising his children's special attributes on birthdays before friends and family.

14. *A servant-leader initiates fun outings for the family on a monthly basis, or even more often.* He keeps laughter in the home!

15. *A servant-leader takes the time to give his children practical instruction about life, which in turn gives them confidence with their peers.* He makes sure they can ride a bike, dribble a basketball, swim, read, and interact meaningfully with the opposite sex, to name just a few. He helps them to feel adequate in life.

16. *A servant-leader goes over the upcoming week with his wife to clarify their schedule and anticipate any pressure points.* He listens to her input and concerns.

17. *A servant-leader keeps the family out of debt.* He also makes sure they are saving for the future and giving to the church.

18. *A servant-leader makes sure he and his wife have drawn up a will and arranged a well-conceived plan for their children in case of death.*

19. *A servant-leader lets his children into the interior of his life.* He wants them to know him as a person, not just as a father. He shares his personal thoughts, dreams, feelings, and memories with them.

20. *A servant-leader praises his wife often in public.* He tells others what it is that makes her so special.

21. *A servant-leader explains sex to each child in a way that gives him or her a wholesome perspective.* He uses books and resources to prepare himself for these special occasions.

22. *A servant-leader encourages his wife to grow as an individual.* He helps her develop her gifts, abilities, and interests. He dreams and interacts with her about how she can use those abilities in special ways, both now and in the future.

23. *A servant-leader takes the lead in establishing with his wife clear and well-reasoned convictions* on issues such as alcohol, debt, child discipline, allowable movies and television

programming, and so on. (These and other choices are too often left undefined in today's homes, with serious consequences.)

24. *A servant-leader joins a small group of men who are dedicated to improving their skills as husbands and fathers.* He invites their accountability in this regard.

25. *A servant-leader provides time for his wife to pursue personal interests,* hobbies, exercise, development of specific talents, and so on.

FOR DISCUSSION

1. Read Ephesians 5:22-33. These verses compare the headship of a husband in a marriage relationship to the headship of Christ with the church. How does this comparison speak to you as a husband? What does your wife see in these verses that impacts her?

2. Reread Luke 22:25-27. Do these verses in any way change your view of "headship"? Why or why not?

3. Discuss the term "servant-leader" again. As you continue studying the husband's role in a marriage, do you think servant-leader is an appropriate term for husbands? Why or why not?

4. Answer the following questions individually first and then share your thoughts with each other: Husbands, can your wife honestly call you servant-leader? If not, what words would she use to describe you? Wives, can you honestly call your husband a servant-leader in your marriage and home? If not, what words would you use to describe him?

5. As a servant-leader, affirm your wife's strengths and assets by listing three positive traits your wife brings to your marriage. How have these gifts impacted your marriage and family?

6. Read through the list below. Husbands, rate yourself. Wives, rate your husband. Use a scale of 1-5 where:

    5=Always **4**=Often **3**=Sometimes **2**=Rarely **1**=Never

    __ __ 1. I include my wife in envisioning the future.
    __ __ 2. I accept spiritual responsibility for my family.
    __ __ 3. I'm willing to say "I'm sorry" and "forgive me" to my family.

___ ___ 4. I discuss household responsibilities with my wife and make sure they're fairly distributed.

___ ___ 5. I seek the consultation of my wife on all major financial decisions.

___ ___ 6. I follow through with commitments I make to my wife.

___ ___ 7. I try to anticipate the different stages my marriage will pass through.

___ ___ 8. Likewise, I try to anticipate the stages my children will pass through and work with my wife to make changes to keep our parenting relevant and effective.

___ ___ 9. I frequently tell my wife what I like about her.

___ ___ 10. I provide financially for my family's basic living expenses.

___ ___ 11. I put aside distractions so that I can talk with my wife and family.

___ ___ 12. I pray with my wife on a regular basis.

___ ___ 13. I try to initiate meaningful family traditions.

___ ___ 14. I try to initiate fun outings for my family at least on a monthly basis.

___ ___ 15. I take the time to give my children practical instruction about life.

___ ___ 16. I take time to go over the upcoming week with my wife to clarify our schedule and anticipate any pressure points.

___ ___ 17. I work to keep our family out of debt.

___ ___ 18. I've made sure that my wife and I have drawn up wills and arranged for our children's care in case of death.

___ ___ 19. I work to let my kids into my life.

___ ___ 20. I praise my wife often in public.

___ ___ 21. I explain sex to each child in a way that gives him or her a wholesome perspective.

___ ___ 22. I encourage my wife to grow as an individual.

___ ___ 23. I take the lead in establishing with my wife clear and well-reasoned convictions on issues such as alcohol, debt, child discipline, allowable movies and television programming, and so on.

___ ___ 24. I belong to a small group of men who are dedicated to improving their skills as husbands and fathers.

__ __ 25. I provide time for my wife to pursue personal interests, hobbies, exercise, development of specific talents, and so on.

When you're finished, add up your scores.

120-125
Score yourself again, (No husband is that perfect!).

100-120
Doing good. Talk through with your wife the areas in which you can still improve.

75-100
You're trying, but you have some work to do. Discuss where and how you can make improvements as a servant-leader.

50-75
Maybe you're not really trying, or you have some wrong ideas about being a servant-leader. The fact that you're going through this book and discussing these things with your wife is a good start. Read this part again. Talk through with your wife any misconceptions you have about what it means to be a servant-leader.

50 or less
Ouch! You may have been raised with some incorrect ideas about the husband's role in marriage. As you continue reading through the book and as you learn more about the wife's role in marriage, think about how you need to reshape your attitude regarding the roles in a marriage. Take this test again in a month, and see if your score goes up.

No matter how you scored, discuss where you differed with your wife's assessment of how you're fulfilling your role and settle on ways you can enhance your servant-leadership!

Part Three

THE HUSBAND'S CORE CONCERNS

Servant
Leader

Security
Significance
Companionship
Emotional Responsiveness

9
Feminine Understanding

Perhaps you've heard the story of a man who phoned a local armory and spoke to a young recruit. "What kind of stock do we have there at the armory, private?" the caller asked authoritatively.

The private replied, "Sir, we have six tanks, six trucks, twelve jeeps, and a whole lot of guns and ammunition. Oh, yeah, we've also got two Cadillacs for our big, fat generals."

The caller paused before barking out, "Private, do you know who this is?"

"No, sir," the startled private replied.

"This is General Weston!"

Again there was a pause in the conversation, until the private asked, "General Weston, do you know who this is?"

Surprised, the general answered, "No!"

The private chuckled and said, "See ya around, fatty!"

HANDLE WITH CARE!

Obviously, it's important to know who you're dealing with! That's especially true when it comes to marriage. Women often baffle us men. So in 1 Peter 3:7, Scripture challenges us with the following exhortation:

> You husbands likewise, live with your wives in an under-
> standing way, as with a weaker vessel, since she is a woman;
> and grant her honor as a fellow heir of the grace of life.

Actually, when Peter tells us to live with our wives "in an understanding way," he literally means, "according to knowledge." In other words, know your wife! Understand she's very different from you. Besides the obvious physical differences, there are vast psychological and emotional differences as well. Don't operate on hearsay, stereotypes, or guesswork. Find out the facts, and treat your wife appropriately.

Notice Peter also tells us how to treat our wives: "as with a weaker vessel." Typically, men read that as, "I have to go easy with my wife. I have to walk on eggshells around her. She can't take much. She's just a fragile little thing." That, I'm afraid, misses the point that Peter is making.

When Peter describes the woman as a "weaker vessel," he's talking about something rare and delicately crafted. A good metaphor is the fine china that your wife keeps hidden away until guests come over. Would you throw your fine china around like paper plates? No! You treat fine china very carefully, not just because it's delicate, *but because it's valuable!* In the same way, you need to treat your wife as the most valuable asset in your home. She's the fine china that God has placed in your life as a gift.

UNDERSTANDING A WOMAN

You treat your wife with care, Peter says, because she is a woman. What a simple but profound statement that is: *since she is a woman.* In other words, she's not a man! You are to treat your wife with different, special care because she is a different, special person. This, by the way, is one of the most powerful phrases in the New Testament in recognizing the distinction between men and women. Because she is a woman, your wife is very different from you as a man. She has different needs, a different perspective, a different way of dealing with the world, and different interests.

Take the area of sex, for instance. Years ago I read in a magazine survey that sex was a man's number-one leisure activity. If you're a man, that's no real surprise, is it? However, that same survey revealed that reading was the number-one leisure activity for women. That's right, reading! Can you believe it, men? We are that different!

It's for reasons like this you are to live with your wife "in an understanding way." Do you know any man who claims to "understand" his wife? If so, have him call me! Psychologically, emotionally, and physically, women manage to confound men at times, creating no end of confusion and consternation.

Yet Peter challenges us to overcome that frustration by learning to treat our wives "according to knowledge." Most men are not necessarily unwilling to meet their wife's needs; they simply are unaware of what those needs really are. For instance, a lot of us assume that what is important to us as men will be important to our wives as well. I couldn't help but laugh when I read the following testimonial:

> Women are very touchy about certain gifts, as I discovered years ago after buying my girlfriend a catcher's mitt for her birthday. It seemed to me to be a particularly thoughtful gift, especially since she claimed not to be getting enough exercise. But apparently she didn't see it that way. The minute she unwrapped it, she ran sobbing from the room.
>
> At first I thought those were tears of joy streaming down her face. I figured she was overwhelmed at being the first in her crowd to have a catcher's mitt, that sort of thing.
>
> Or I figured she was so excited she couldn't wait to get outside and work on her throws to second base. But when she didn't return after a few hours, I got the hint. . . .
>
> Here I'd spent all that time running from one sporting goods store to the next, just to find the perfect gift—we're talking a Johnny Bench model here, top of the line—and she calls me "insensitive."
>
> Go figure, right? I mean, you'd think I gave her a year's subscription to "Field and Stream." Or a box of shotgun shells, which everybody knows should be saved for Christmas stocking stuffers.

Personally, I think she just had a lot of anger in her and took it out on me, not that I'm trying to play amateur psychologist. . . .

Anyway, good luck. When she starts swinging, I mean.[1]

I think every man has made that mistake in one way or another. Not long ago I gave my wife a two-year membership to a health club for Christmas. Of course, I assumed (wrongly!) that because I liked to work out at a health club, she would, too. Well, after I made the twenty-fourth payment on a completely unused membership, it finally occurred to me that I'd misinterpreted her needs!

Many times, however, it ceases to be funny. As one psychologist explained, "A man can have the best of intentions to meet his wife's needs, but if he thinks her needs are similar to his own, he will fail miserably."[2] Some of us men really do fail miserably. We're shooting in the dark when it comes to understanding our wives. And it hurts. No wonder so many marriages have fallen on hard times. As a pastor I often hear men boil over and say something like, "I don't know what she wants from me! I can't please her! I knock myself out twelve hours a day to give her everything anyone could ever want, and she still isn't satisfied! What's the deal?"

I'm going to devote the next chapter to "the deal." But for now it's worth noting that you can meet your wife's wants yet still miss her needs. That's what the deal is. Your wife doesn't *need* you to work twelve hours a day. More likely, it's you who "needs" to work that much. You're out there trying to find your identity and establish your worth and value. You're out there for you more than for her. What she needs is for you "to live with her in an understanding way . . . *since* she is a woman"! A little feminine understanding can go a long way in meeting your wife's real needs.

So, what are those real needs? Let's find out.

10

What Every Wife Needs to Succeed

Do you want to live with your wife "in an understanding way"? Then read the following pages carefully. I want to offer four important terms worth remembering that could forever change your relationship with your wife. These terms represent four all-important needs that your wife has. She has other needs beyond these four, of course. But none of them affects the nature and quality of your marriage as profoundly as these. They are keys to her happiness in marriage. They should be your *core* concerns as a husband.

COMPANIONSHIP

The first need your wife has is *companionship*. As a woman, your wife was made by God out of high-intensity relational material. In marriage, much of her identity and sense of worth come from how well she relates to you.

Have you ever wondered why soap operas are so popular, even addictive, to many homemakers? Have you ever noticed how many romance novels are targeted toward women in supermarkets and bookstores? Those things feed on a woman's powerful need for companionship. They create a fantasy that supplies what she may lack in real life. In a powerful way, they exploit her imagination, conjuring up all kinds of highly romantic images in which two people deeply experience one another's lives.

Have you ever watched a soap opera, men? It just goes on and on and on, day after day after day. Over time, you get to know all the characters—all their feelings, thoughts, motives, ambitions, failures. In fact, *everything* about them is exposed. And it never ends, does it? The revelations just keep going deeper and deeper.

There's a powerful lesson here: That's exactly how most women desire to relate to their husbands. They seek to experience life with their men in a deep, intimate, never-ending way. There's no particular goal in mind; they just want to cherish the experience of the relationship. *Being* is more satisfying than *doing*. That mystifies most men.

It shouldn't be that strange to us! Men, remember the days of courtship? Remember how you blocked out everything else and gave full attention to your sweetheart? You did all kinds of crazy things to make time to spend with her, didn't you? You read and reread her letters, and when you finished, you read them all over again, analyzing every word, deciphering every nuance and shade of meaning. You shared out of the depth of your soul special things about you and her. You were also free about sharing your feelings and your dreams. And your honey loved and relished every minute of it! In you, she found what she wanted—deep companionship. Unfortunately, when the ceremony is over, the honeymoon is complete, and married life actually begins, our masculine efforts at deep and abiding companionship all too often wither.

I once saw a Valentine that expressed this transformation well. The front panel drips with hyper-romantic sentiment: "If you love something, set it free. If it returns, you haven't lost it. If it disappears and never comes back, then it wasn't truly yours to begin with." Inside, the message concludes, "And if it just sits there watching television, unaware that it's been set free, then you probably married it."

If you've been married for any length of time, you know how the expectations that began in courtship are so easily disappointed once the wedding bells stop ringing. A woman views the wedding ceremony as the beginning of a never-ending relationship with a lot of deep sharing. But the man sees it in terms of completing a goal. "We did it!" After the ceremony is over, he's ready to move on to other things, *especially* his career. For a wife, this brings unexpected disappointment and heartache.

The more he focuses on interests outside the home, the more his wife hungers to have him back, to share in his experiences, to have him to be with. She wants to talk with him about the things going on in his life, to keep in touch, to enjoy the conversation of companionship. She may want to go shopping with him, not necessarily to buy something, but just to wander around the mall together, enjoying each other's company. That's likely to drive him crazy! He wants to get in and get out, and do it in record time! He wants to check it off his list of chores and go on to the next thing.

Men, when you take time to "be" with your wife, you're paying her the supreme compliment. You're telling her how important she is to you. You're expressing your commitment to her. You're letting her know that you enjoy her and enjoy being *with* her. Listen—your wife yearns for that! It's what she expected when you placed that ring on her finger. When you were married, she took your name, and that in itself says a great deal about what she expects. More than anything else, she expects to have *you*—your presence, your interest, your availability. She wants and needs your companionship.

SECURITY

A second need your wife has is *security*. It's interesting that there is almost universal contempt for men who look to their wives for protection or provision. But it's natural for women to expect that from their husbands. Of course, as many as one-fifth of all dual-earner couples today have wives earning more than husbands, so it would be easy to assume that their jobs provide all the security they need.[1] It doesn't work that way. A woman needs the security of a man. She needs to know he can and will provide for her.

Whether or not your wife is employed outside the home is not the point. Rather, a wife needs to feel secure and able to rest in the certainty that she would be secure whether she worked or not. She needs to feel confident that she has a man looking out for her. So husbands, let me ask you: Have you made your marriage financially sound? Does it offer real security for your wife? Can she trust you? Are your finances under control? Biblically, these things are your responsibility.[2]

I'm amazed at how many men today are shirking or abandoning their duties here. The vast majority of people who fall below the poverty level in this country are women and children. Where are their men? Who gave these men the right to neglect or walk away from their commitments, leaving behind single mothers to pick up the pieces? Conversely, who said it was okay for successful white-collar men to pursue younger women, plunging their wives and children into emotional and financial catastrophe?

It's time for someone to stand up and say this is wrong! It's out of line! This is a violation of God's clear-cut orders! It certainly is out of bounds for any man who claims to be a Christian. And I believe churches need to take a far tougher stance in calling men to accountability for such irresponsible behavior. This is certainly the New Testament perspective:

> If anyone does not provide for his own, and especially for those of his own household, he has denied the faith, and is worse than an unbeliever. (1 Timothy 5:8)

At the same time, we need to affirm men who do provide for their families. We need to honor them for that effort. I have set for myself the goal that my wife should never *have* to work. She may *choose* to, but she shouldn't have to. It should be an option for her, not a necessity. I realize, of course, that there are some situations today where that's not possible, and wives must work. But if men felt more responsibility for meeting the financial security needs of their families, these situations would be exceptions, not a growing national trend.

SIGNIFICANCE

A third major need your wife has is *significance*. Why? Because so much of what she does is hidden from view. Her most valuable contributions are primarily relational. She's a nurturer, a friend, a soul-worker. These contributions can't be measured quantitatively. Nor will she get paid for them.

The only person who can really appreciate her unique contributions, the only one who can honor her accordingly, is you, her husband. That's why in 1 Peter 3:7, Peter exhorts a husband to grant to his wife "honor." That's right, honor! If you don't praise and exalt her, who will? Who else knows and values what your wife does during the day? Your children don't fully perceive it, and they certainly aren't inclined to thank her for it. The neighbors don't know. If she holds a job, her employer cares mainly about her performance at work. Your employer, on the other hand, cares mainly about her impact on your work. Society pays little attention to her contributions in the home. So who is there to praise and compliment her for her value and importance as a wife and mother? No one except you! You're the only one.

The tragedy is that over the last forty years, so many women have felt unappreciated and insignificant in serving their families that they've given up on it. "It's not worth it," they're saying; "we're going elsewhere to find our sense of significance."

A 1970 Roper poll found that two-thirds of women in the United States agreed with the statement that "most men are basically kind, gentle, and thoughtful." But a 1990 repeat poll discovered that only half of the women agreed. In fact, 42 percent described men as "basically selfish and self-centered." Fifty-three percent said that "most men are interested in their work and life outside the home and don't pay much attention to things going on at home." That feeling was up from 39 percent in 1970.[3]

If the truth were known, money is not the sole driving force behind women entering the workforce today. It's a factor, to be sure. But for many, if not most, the psychological rewards of paid work are making up for a deficit of the praise husbands should have been giving all along.

It's hard to fault a woman for wanting to feel significant. Every person needs to know that she matters, that her life counts. By the way, does your wife know that? If you're not affirming her on a daily basis, I guarantee she doesn't—not the way she needs to.

EMOTIONAL RESPONSIVENESS

Finally, your wife has a need for you to be *emotionally responsive* to her. Her world is one of deep feelings. When Sherard tells me that she's "down" or "upset," my natural response is to try to solve her problem.

When I do, she says, "You just don't understand!" She's right. What I don't understand is that most of the time she doesn't want me to solve anything for her. She just wants me to listen. As author John Gray writes, "When a man does not object to or argue with a woman's feeling, but instead accepts and confirms their validity, and listens with empathy as she explores those feelings, a woman will feel truly loved."[4]

Of course, you haven't solved her problem, but you've done the right thing. You've experienced her world, and that's what she needs most from you. It's a revolutionary husband who says, "Tell me about it, honey" and listens, rather than saying, "You shouldn't be bringing that up again! Get over it!" or "What you need is more sleep," or "Don't you think you're letting this get to you too much?"

More than a century ago, Dinah Craick spoke for wives who yearn for, and desire a husband's emotional responsiveness when she wrote:

> *Oh, the comfort, the inexpressible comfort*
> *Of feeling safe with another person;*
> *Having neither to weigh thoughts*
> *Or measure words,*
> *But pouring them all right out*
> *Just as they are,*
> *Certain that a faithful hand can and*
> *Will take them.*

That's our job, husbands.

A servant-leader is committed to meeting these special needs his wife possesses as a woman. If he's wise, he'll make the issues of companionship, security, significance, and emotional responsiveness his core concerns. Nothing could make his wife happier!

For Discussion

1. Read 1 Peter 3:7. List some of the key words he uses here to describe how husbands should treat their wives, and define them in your own words. Now discuss with your spouse if and how those meanings get lived out in your marriage.

2. What do you think Peter means when he concludes the verse by saying, "so that nothing will hinder your prayers"? Read Matthew 5:23-24. Husbands, have you ever sensed your relationship with God weakening at times when you're not honoring and respecting your wife? How do these verses in Matthew command you to handle this situation?

3. This section used four key words to describe what wives need to succeed in marriage. Husbands and wives, each of you define these terms in your own words: companionship, security, significance, and emotional responsiveness.

4. Husbands, can you think of one special way that you can show your wife that you are committed to being her life-long companion? What's the clearest way you can demonstrate to her that you want to provide for her security? What's the best way you can show her that her role as wife and mother is the most significant thing she can do with her life? How can you more appropriately respond to her emotionally centered concerns?

    Wives, think through these same questions: How can your husband show his commitment to you? How can he make you feel more secure? How can he let you know how significant your role is in your family and marriage? How can he respond to your emotion-based worries and concerns? Discuss your ideas and give each other feedback.

Part Four

THE WIFE'S CORE ROLE

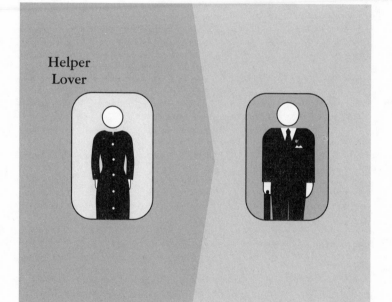

Helper
Lover

11

What's a Woman to Choose?

I don't envy you if you're a woman today. You have so much to choose from and so many hard choices. In a small way, I can identify with your predicament. It's hard to imagine now, but there was a time when a number of colleges and universities were fiercely competing for my athletic abilities. Being courted at seventeen by recruiters from Louisiana State University, University of Arkansas, Ole' Miss, Southern Methodist University, and others was an absolutely dizzying experience. Overwhelming! Every one of them sounded wonderful.

By signing day, I was so confused that I decided the only thing I could do was guess. So, being from Louisiana, I called LSU and told the head coach I was ready to sign. He was thrilled and in a matter of hours was on his way north from Baton Rouge with a group of reporters for the signing.

While his plane was still in the air, Frank Broyles called from the University of Arkansas. Our conversation left me paralyzed. Soon after, a parade of LSU coaches with scholarship in-hand arrived to celebrate my commitment. This should have been one of the great moments in my life, but instead it was one of the most embarrassing. I couldn't bring myself to sign. All I could say was, "I'm sorry. I can't do it!" As you can imagine, they were outraged! They kept asking,

"Why? Why?" But I had no solid answers. I wasn't even sure why myself. There were just too many options, and I had no way of measuring with any certainty which one would be best for me.

Today's woman faces the same dilemma. Many of the barriers that once restricted women to narrowly defined roles have been removed. It can be said that every field is now within a woman's reach. The options are endless.

For a while, women were told they could "do it all." "Super Moms" and "Super Women," they were called. But it turned out to be a "Super Myth." One woman told me, "I'm spread so thin right now, I don't know if there's anything left to devote to anything else. I'm an overworked professional, an overtired mother, a part-time wife, and a fair-weather friend!" The promise of having it all has led many women to a great deal of exhaustion, guilt, and heartache.

So if she can't have it all, what's a woman to choose? What are the priorities? What things does she let go of?

OPPORTUNITY OVERLOAD

A few years ago *USA Today* reported on a poll that *Family Circle* magazine conducted among 35,000 of its readers. The periodical wanted to know what women were letting go of to make their lives more bearable. They found that housework was the first thing to go. More than 50 percent said their standards for housework had fallen. Fifty-one percent said they squeezed out friends; 25 percent said they neglected their husbands; 75 percent said their sex life had suffered. The article summarized, "When strapped for time, busy women push friends, housework, husbands, and sex to life's back burner."[1] Is there anything today's woman won't let go of? The poll found just two things—a job outside the home and children. Yet the most stressed-out and time-pressed woman of all, according to this report, was a woman working full-time with one young child at home.

In the midst of so many opportunities and choices for women, one option seems clearly to be vanishing: the full-time housewife. It's a new day for women with new deals and options, options, and more options. So, what's a woman to choose? How can she make choices that are more than guesswork?

When I was seventeen, trying to decide on a college, I could have used some dependable guidelines. Looking back, I now realize I could have gone to some of the finest schools in the country academically. But my parents and I didn't have the larger perspective on my opportunities. No one was there to help us see how that choice would affect my later choices in life, or how it could be a steppingstone to what I might want to achieve later. So after all the recruiting wars were over, including the LSU debacle, my decision was still just a guess. I picked Arkansas, but I couldn't explain my reasons. It just *seemed* right.

Women, you cannot afford to guess when it comes to what role you play in your home. You're too important to your husband. You're too needed by your family. You cannot afford to guess your life away in the midst of so many pressing opportunities that clamor for your allegiance. Many have done so and guessed wrong, to their great regret. Such are the dangers.

Clearly, you need guidelines — not rules, not straitjackets, but precepts and principles that empower you to develop a wise decision-making process. You also need to know your role.

The Bible offers both. It shows that God wants your marriage to be a beautiful symbiotic relationship in which you and your husband play complementary, mutually supportive, and satisfying roles. In part 2, we saw that your husband's role is to be a *servant-leader,* a man who showers you with Christlike love and honor. What, then, is your role as a wife?

GODLY GUIDELINES
The circumstances of Titus 2 return to a period in the Roman Empire when the institution of marriage was in dramatic retreat. In a remarkable parallel to today, women were throwing off all the traditional restraints that had bound them. The home had become only one option among many. Therefore, Paul's words in this letter to a young pastor named Titus must be understood in light of this cultural backdrop:

> As for you, speak the things which are fitting for sound doctrine. Older men are to be temperate, dignified, sensible,

sound in faith, in love, in perseverance. Older women, likewise are to be reverent in their behavior, . . . teaching what is
good, that they may encourage the younger women to love
their husbands, to love their children, to be sensible, pure,
workers at home, kind, being subject to their own husbands,
that the word of God may not be dishonored. (Titus 2:1-5)

Notice Paul's opening words. They form an important pream-
ble to the directions that follow. Paul is not asking Titus to give
guidelines that fit the prevailing culture. Rather, his guidelines
should fit with sound doctrine—that is, the Word of God. With
that opening, he then shows how older men should act and how
older women should conduct themselves. But in addition to these
measures of maturity, notice Paul calls on the older women to
encourage their younger counterparts to specific action.

Why did these younger women need encouragement in regard
to their husband, children, and home? For one thing, the culture
was lessening the importance of these things. For another, those
younger women were being tempted with new opportunities and
options that would make loving a husband or raising children
extremely difficult. These young women needed the insight of
wise, mature women to sort out real priorities from vain pursuits
that would turn sour later. There is nothing more helpful than the
solid experience of someone you respect to help you make choices
you won't regret later.

A WOMAN'S CORE ROLE

I believe this list of responsibilities in Titus 2:4-5 represents the
most succinct summary of a woman's *core* role in all of Scripture.
This defines the term *helper* (the title given by God to Eve in
Genesis 2:18) in clear and specific terms. We'll pay close attention
to two of these responsibilities in the next chapter.

For now, let's remind ourselves that a core role is not everything a woman does in marriage. She is not confined only to what
Paul describes here. But she dare not excuse herself from these
responsibilities or neglect them for other ambitions. Like the plan-
ets around the sun, everything in marriage should revolve around

these crucial core-role responsibilities and concerns. A wife's core role should prioritize her commitments and her use of energy and time. It should keep her from missing out on what God has called her to do in her life and in her marriage.

It also should give stability to her marriage because it provides a grid through which she can filter, measure, and evaluate all the opportunities that come her way. Unfortunately, the mistake many women are making today is in treating these core-role responsibilities as just options in a myriad of options. But a core role is not an option. It's a biblical absolute.

Notice that Paul issues a strong warning in the Titus passage. To ignore or treat these responsibilities lightly is to dishonor the Word of God. When a great number of women ignore their core role, or substitute other roles for it, society will certainly begin to reflect that loss. Families will unravel. Marriages will break down. Such was the case in the Roman Empire, and such is the case in our own society today.

Needless to say, a woman has an incredibly important role to play in her marriage! She's absolutely indispensable. So much depends on whether she plays her part well. So let's turn to the specific details involved in her assignment.

12

Husband-Lover and Child-Lover

Again, let me say that the most challenging passage of Scripture I
know for today's Christian woman is Titus 2:4-5. Here, spelled out
in the clearest terms possible, are her primary, "core" responsibilities in marriage:

> Encourage the young women to love their husbands, to love
> their children, to be sensible, pure, workers at home, kind,
> being subject to their own husbands, that the word of God
> may not be dishonored.

In this chapter I'll examine only the first two phrases of this
definitive statement. In the first, "to love their husbands," Paul
actually uses a single word: *husband-lover*. A wife is to be a
husband-lover.

A HUSBAND-LOVER

Does it seem obvious that a wife should love her husband? It
wasn't in first-century Crete, where Titus was. Nor was it in many
other parts of the Roman Empire. Remember, many women in
those times looked outside the home for other pursuits. They took
all sorts of jobs, which in turn took time and energy. No doubt in

the crunch of "other things," those women did what the *Family Circle* poll said women are doing today: They probably pushed their husbands and their sex lives to the back burner, too. Their husbands lost out on both counts. They lost the stabilizing support a wife can give, and they lost the rich affirmation a healthy sex life provides.

Husband-lover—the roots of that responsibility go all the way back to Genesis 2:18, to the account of the creation of woman. After creating Adam, the male, God made the following evaluation:

> Then the Lord God said, "It is not good for the man to be alone; I will make him a helper suitable for him."

Notice that woman was conceived *out* of the need of man. This doesn't mean that she was somehow secondary, or that she was created as an afterthought.[1] No, when God made this statement, He showed that He has a specific purpose in mind for woman. Her support is essential to man's success. Therefore, the woman's creation both exposed a great need within man and at the same time met it.

WHAT IS A "HELPER"?

Wives, God has made you to be a "suitable helper" to your husband. That's a fascinating term, but widely misunderstood. To modern Americans, a "helper" is a subordinate, an assistant, a "gofer." Helpers do the dirty work. They have no authority. They just tag along, waiting for someone important to tell them what to do.

But that's not what the original readers of Genesis thought of when they read this word. Far from it! In nearly every other instance in the Old Testament, when this word for "helper" or "help" is used, it refers to God and the help that He supplies, particularly as a defense against adversaries.[2] For instance, in several places, God is described as "our help and our shield."[3] One passage describes Him helping David by strengthening him to become king over Israel.[4] And consider the famous opening to Psalm 121:1-2 (NIV):

I lift up my eyes to the hills—
where does my help come from?

My help comes from the Lord,
the Maker of heaven and earth.

If the Maker of Heaven and earth is a helper, I think it's clear that there is no shame in being a helper.[5] In fact, in the context of the Old Testament, it appears that a "helper" is a strong person who supports and provides assistance to a weaker person, or someone in real need. I don't want to get into a debate here on whether women at some points are stronger than men or vice versa. I'm just trying to make the point that there is no implication of weakness or inferiority in the woman's role as "helper." In fact, I wish we had a better English word to use because the idea of subordination has become so attached to *helper.*

In 1 Corinthians 11:9, Paul says it this way:

For indeed man was not created for the woman's sake, but woman for the man's sake.

Again, that's not a putdown; it's a tremendous compliment to you as a woman. You are invaluable to your man. He needs someone custom-made to help him be and do what he can't be and do by himself. Your support is essential to his success. Without your focus, attention, and encouragement, he'll have glaring gaps in his life. It's not good for a husband to be left alone.

Yet that's exactly what's happening today! With so many options and interests, many wives have become too pressed for time and too emotionally drained to give much attention to their husbands. They are ignoring some of the very supports that men need most, supports they can't do without. Many overworked, overstressed wives have become half-mates to their husbands rather than help-mates.

Fighting on Two Fronts

Let me illustrate by describing what happened to the Germans in World War II. Germany enjoyed some stunning victories, conquering the Czechs, the Poles, the Austrians, and even the French. They were on the verge of taking England when Hitler became greedy and decided to open up a second front by attacking Russia. It was a perilous mistake. Soon his armies were overextended. Support lines grew so thin that they could not replenish what was being used up. So they ran out of bullets. They ran out of food. And finally, they ran out of gas. This one blunder cost the Germans hundreds of thousands of lives — and the war.

In many homes today, young couples are making the same mistake. They're trying to fight on two fronts, and it's proving costly. Too costly. On one front, both husband and wife hold down full-time jobs outside the home. Meanwhile, responsibilities at home pose a second front. Neither "battle" is going well. Both partners are tired and exhausted. Their overextended "supply lines" have become extremely thin. They look to each other with open, needy hands, seeking help, but neither one has anything left with which to comfort the other. There is no support. No wonder immorality rises dramatically in that kind of environment. Needy people, out of gas, often look elsewhere for someone to refuel them.

The issue here is not whether you as a wife should or should not work outside the home. Rather, the question is where your primary focus should be. Genesis 2, 1 Corinthians 11, and Titus 2, among other passages, indicate that it should be on your husband. God has given you the awesome responsibility of supporting and helping him. The power to accomplish this calling is quite simple. I call it the power of being there — that's right, being there. Being available to him, giving him time, energy, and priority. Giving thought and creativity to building him up. Just being there for your husband is an incredible source of strength to him. It's life-giving! If you don't think your man needs that kind of support, I suggest you may be blind to what's really going on in him.

In Proverbs 31 we find a portrait of "the excellent wife," the woman who pursues this high and holy calling of "husband-lover." It tells us why she has placed this pursuit above so many others. At the end of the chapter (verse 30), we find that she "fears the Lord." Not society. Not her friends and what they might think of her. Not her associates at work. No, she fears the Lord. She's concerned with what He thinks. She marches to a different drumbeat from her peers by choosing to honor God's Word. More than anything else, she wants to be right with God.

A CHILD-LOVER

However, your core role as a woman doesn't stop there. Titus 2:4 goes on to encourage you to be a *child-lover.* This responsibility is also a single word. Again, I find it amazing that women would have to be encouraged to love children. In our own day it seems that more and more women view children as an imposition rather than a gift, as a liability rather than an asset. Yet, I'm afraid that fighting against the maternal instinct is like trying to shut off Niagara Falls. It's not only unnatural, it's virtually impossible.[6] It's also unbiblical (see Genesis 1:28).

Children, especially young ones, need tremendous doses of personal attention, support, and of course, love. Children need the awesome power of "being there" to be unleashed on them, too. You see, it's not good for a child to be alone either.

Seven-year-old Brian wrote Dr. James Dobson the following note: "Dear Dr. Dobson, I have a working mom and a working dad and I would like to know what us kids can do."[7]

The research on this need is overwhelming. But suffice it to say, according to many childcare experts, healthy, normal child development requires a close, loving, and sustained relationship with at least one person during a minimum of the first two years of life.[8] Titus 2 indicates that the mother should provide that. Without mom exercising the power of "being there" for her children, the next generation will be even more dysfunctional than this present one.

In practice this means that if you are a mother with younger children, you belong at home with your children more than you belong outside the home at work. I know there are single mothers for whom that is virtually impossible and there are families struggling to make ends meet, where mothers have to work. And of course there have been many cultures throughout history and around the world today where women work in addition to raising children. I'm well aware of these situations that would seem to contradict the notion of "full-time" mothers.

But I want to point out that there is a major-league difference between mothers with young children who *must* work out of financial necessity, and those who *choose* to work *as an alternative to mothering*. And I believe children know this difference, too! This is a complex issue, with many angles to consider. But in the spirit of Titus 2, I want to encourage you, if you are a mother with young children, to devote yourself to your children during their first critical, formative years. Career opportunities will *always* be there.[9] But children grow up only *once*. Can you afford to forgo that once-in-a-lifetime investment?

I'll have much more to say about this issue in chapters 24 and 26. There, I'll clarify and qualify my position. For now, I want to stress that Scripture certainly doesn't prohibit you from working outside the home. But you need biblical guidelines and perspectives. Don't just live by guesswork; think it through according to the Word of God.

Your core role as a wife, then, is to be a husband-lover and a child-lover. They need your touch and your support to stabilize and energize their lives. So, please, for their sakes, *be there!*

FOR DISCUSSION

1. Read Genesis 2:18 and Titus 2:4-5. What these verses say is the core role of the wife in marriage. What are some ways this role gets overlooked? What do you think happens to the marriage relationship when this role breaks down?
2. Read Proverbs 31:10-31. List the qualities found in these verses. What do you think today's society would think of this list? Discuss what your response should be when a biblical calling conflicts with what society seems to be saying.
3. Think about the term "helper-lover," and define this word in your own terms. Do you think helper-lover is an appropriate term for wives?
4. Wives, can your husband honestly call you a helper-lover? If not, what words might he use instead to describe you?

   Husbands, can you honestly call your wife a helper-lover in your marriage and home? If not, what words would you use to describe her? Now share your thoughts with each other. Talk about ways the wife can be more of a helper. In what ways can she be more of a lover. Husbands, what are some ways you can encourage your wife to completely assume this role in your marriage?

Part Five

THE WIFE'S CORE CONCERNS

Helper
Lover

Support
Admiration
Companionship
Physical Responsiveness

13

Getting into a Man's Head

The world of men is a mystery to most women. Dr. Joyce Brothers writes, "Most of the questions I am asked after lectures and television appearances are not about women but about men. If I have heard it once, I have heard it a thousand and one times . . . that half-furious, half-humorous complaint, 'I just don't understand that man!'"[1]

The fact is, men *are* a mystery—not only to women, but to themselves as well. Most men are not especially eager to think deeply about themselves, so they give their wives only a meager amount of information to go on. For a wife who wants to enjoy her man and share life intimately with him, this can be extremely frustrating.

In this chapter and the next, I want to demystify some of the "masculine mystique" that men seem to hide behind. The place to begin is the brain. Wives, if you want to understand your husband, you need to get inside his head!

YOU KNEW IT ALL ALONG

Did you know that the male brain is *physically* different from the female brain? The two have different shapes, and the same parts do certain things differently. In fact, these differences show up even before birth.[2]

The male and female brains also function differently. This has been demonstrated from the fascinating studies of right-brain and left-brain activity. Though this field is in its infancy, already some intriguing findings have come forth.

For instance, in the male brain, the right and left hemispheres typically work independently of one another. Men usually emphasize one side of their brain over the other. That may explain why men tend to be such *focused* creatures. By "shutting down" one side of the brain, they can shut out distractions.

By contrast, the two sides of the female brain operate together, on an integrative, wholistic level. Some experts have described a woman's brain as being much like a high-speed computer. They can drink in instantly all that's going on around them, which often brings them to conclusions they can't explain. What we call "woman's intuition" is in reality a high-speed, integrative thought process. In short, women's brains are like radar; men's brains are more like laser beams.

Now these are not hard and fast rules. The research is still very primitive. But awareness of these differences has helped some wives become more tolerant and understanding of their husbands. It has caused them to reassess their criticisms of certain annoying male habits women so often complain about. For example, take the way a man can "tune out" his wife. Every woman has felt that from time to time. You find your husband in the living room opening his mail. Thinking he's available, you begin to pour your heart out to him. As you go on and on, he makes an occasional grunt or two to let you know that he's aware you're there. But then it becomes obvious he's not with you at all—he's with his mail! You feel hurt, mad, and disgusted.

My wife used to click her fingers in front of my face in those moments and say, "Are you listening?" Her tone made it clear that this was more of an accusation than a question. Quite honestly, I'm not listening. But not for the reason she may think. She may conclude I'm insensitive or, worse, that I don't care. But the reality is, I'm focused. Whether I'm reading the mail, watching television, or whatever, my brain is doing what it was created to do—shut out the distractions and focus.

Now that we have two sons, my wife has discovered I'm not

the only one who has this "focus disease." Knowing this has brought about an "extra tolerance factor" in my wife that is helpful to both of us. She knows when to communicate and when to wait for my attention.

EYES IN THE BACK OF HER HEAD

As a woman, you tend to think much more broadly than a man. You can be focused on one thing and yet aware of the overall landscape at the same time. I'm always amazed at how Sherard can keep track of what's going on all over our house. She'll be in the kitchen baking, focused on a certain recipe, and yet is somehow still able to carry on a conversation with one of our children. Meanwhile, she's in touch with what's going on in the next room with another child *and* with another one upstairs. Don't ask me how she does it! A man's brain simply does not have that kind of power.

I'm awestruck by my wife's ability when we sit as a family around the supper table. She can serve the food while all four of our kids are talking to her at once, and seem perfectly at ease in the midst of the chaos. Not me! I'm hyper-frustrated in those situations. I'm always trying to focus somewhere, on someone, but it's impossible! For a focused male brain, four kids talking at the same time is torture! But not for Sherard. Somehow she can serve a meal *and* carry on a four-way—no—a five-way conversation at the same time. Incredible!

An asset at the supper table can be an annoyance in the bedroom, however. In the intimacy of lovemaking, most women have a real need to feel totally secure. They want to know the door is locked . . . the curtains are closed . . . the windows are bolted . . . the electric fence is on. Security is very important!

Yet, with all kinds of reassurances, a woman's brain will continue to be in touch with all that's going on around her. Her radar is constantly scanning the front lawn, the neighbor's house, and the children's bedrooms upstairs. As a result, in the midst of lovemaking, a wife can ask at the most inopportune moment, "George did you hear that?" (It was probably the refrigerator light going off!)

What makes her question so funny is that she's asking someone whose brain is *not* like hers! She's asking a guy who at that moment is clinically brain-dead in one hemisphere and hyper-focused on a very important goal in the other one. An eighteen-wheeler could drive through the bedroom and he wouldn't notice!

PRODUCT VERSUS PROCESS

Another difference in the way men and women think is that we men tend to limit our focus to essentials. We're bottom-line people. We usually don't try to "feel" an experience as a woman does; we just want to know the results. That can be extremely frustrating to a wife. I'll come home from the church and say to Sherard, "Did you know that Mary had a baby boy today? I saw it posted at church."

Naturally, Sherard gets excited, so she asks, "What's the baby's name?" She wants to start drinking in the experience of this new little life.

"I don't know." (I didn't look.)

"Well, how's Mary doing?" she asks.

"Gee, I don't know. I didn't ask anybody. I guess I didn't think about it."

"Well, do you know when she delivered? How much did the baby weigh? Is he doing okay? Is he healthy? I wonder if anybody's taking meals to Fred and the kids."

A thousand other details pop into her mind, stuff I never even considered. You see, all those are important to her, but that's not what matters to me. It's that Mary did it! She had the baby! She achieved the goal! That's how I tend to think as a man. Give me the bottom-line. Stick to the essentials. In a situation like that, Sherard really has to rely on that "extra tolerance factor" to avoid getting put out with me!

DADDY ISN'T HOME YET!

Let me mention one other area that really bothers women. It's how a husband comes home from work. Most men will seem totally detached at the end of a day. With that glazed stare, they look like they could star in *Night of the Living Dead!* In a very real sense, most men are still at work. It's that "focused factor" again. Men have a hard time breaking their focus. Women really struggle with this. A wife wants her husband to switch gears and join her in the new reality of home and the kids when he walks in the door. She also wants to unload on him her experience from her work and hear about his. But for a man, this changing of mindsets is extremely difficult. No wonder "re-entry" is one of the times of greatest conflict in marriage.

One of my good friends, Barbara Rainey, has realized this about her husband, Dennis, and has cut him some slack in the process. "When Dennis comes home from work detached, I realize . . . he's just being himself—a man!" Can you hear the "extra tolerance factor" in that statement? That's a mature perspective. She goes on: "The children will scream for his attention, yet he doesn't seem to hear them. So, I tell them, 'Relax, kids, Daddy isn't home, yet!' They'll say, 'Yes, he is! Yes, he is! He's standing right here!' But I tell them, '*We* know he's home, but *he* doesn't know it, yet!'" That's a good example of living with your man in an understanding way.

Of course, getting inside a man's head is just the beginning. But it's a great starting point for understanding the man you've chosen to live your life with. It will add patience and compassion to places where perhaps only exasperation reigned. It can also make your marriage ride a whole lot smoother.

There are other factors besides brain differences that can be extremely helpful to you as a woman in knowing your man. These factors touch on the very nature of manhood itself. In the next chapter, I'll suggest three powerful words that will allow you to look deeply inside the masculine soul.

14

What Every Wife Needs to Know About Her Husband

In 1975, Dr. James Dobson authored the book *What Wives Wish Their Husbands Knew About Women.* It became a runaway best seller because it articulated some of the critical needs of women that men simply do not understand. It's still available, by the way, and I encourage every husband to read it.

Now that we're in the nineties, I believe the shoe is on the other foot. I've discovered that there are important needs men have that women either don't understand or are not aware of. Women have lost touch with some of the fundamentals of manhood. As a result, many wives don't "respect" their husbands in the way that Ephesians 5:33 encourages them to do. The problem is that they don't really know how their men are wired.

In this chapter, I'd like to suggest three powerful words that will broaden your understanding of men. I like to think of them as summations of manhood. These words express realities that are behind much of the activity in a man's life.

IDENTITY

The first word is *identity.* What is it that makes a man . . . a man? For that matter, what is it that makes a woman . . . a woman? Besides their obvious physical differences, who are they, really?

If we could strip everything away, where we would have nothing but ourselves and our bodies to observe, what answers do we receive? A woman would observe her body and realize that she has a very obvious calling. She has a menstrual cycle, a uterus, breasts, and so on. All of these point to a role of unquestioned importance, for whatever else she does or doesn't do, *she* is the originator of life! She has that essential purpose. Seymour Fisher, of the National Institute of Health, wrote, "A woman's body 'makes sense' to her. It's one of the prime means to become what she in fact wants to become."[1]

But what identity does a man's body give him? Other than the fact that he has a role in originating life, there's no clear answer, is there? Nothing obvious anyway. This emptiness of ultimate purpose creates a tremendous restlessness within men. Women, on the other hand, are not nearly as insecure. They may pursue all kinds of objectives in a lifetime, but they begin these pursuits already knowing they have a valuable purpose in life. Men have no such flooring. Therefore, they have a tremendous need to define themselves. They have a gigantic question mark hanging over their lives. And they feel driven to discover who they are and why they are needed.

Women wonder why men are always pushing themselves. Behind much of it is a search for a meaningful identity—one that gives some ultimate meaning to life.

Of course, a man can find his ultimate purpose only when he finds Jesus Christ. But wedded very closely to his relationship to Christ are his work and his wife. Together, these three play decisive roles in his life, functioning as keys that unlock the door to his identity.

INSECURITY

That leads us to a second word, *insecurity*. We men will never say we feel insecure, of course. We have to appear strong. In fact, our society asks us to play that role. We always have to look like we have life under control. But deep down, in a way that's very different from women, we are a very fragile and insecure bunch. We are never quite sure about ourselves, or whether we are in the right place. Not really.

Many women complain that their husbands just can't relax. "He's always pushing and driving himself," a wife will say. I feel that way, even when I have a day off. I'll have absolutely nothing to do, which terrorizes me. I have to get up and make something happen. My wife will say, "Hey, why don't you just sit down and relax?" Part of me wishes that I could. But for me, even rest is often defined in terms of *doing* something. I'm convinced that underneath all this hyperactivity, for myself and others, is a sex that is deeply insecure.

As George Gilder said in his acclaimed book *Men and Marriage,* "A man's body is full of undefined energies only. For him, manhood is made. It is not born."[2] So, all through his life a man tries to define himself. He aggressively seeks some meaningful validation. In junior high or high school, he might try to do it through athletics or academic achievement. In college, some guys party harder than everyone else, as if that will establish their sense of manhood. In the work world, a man may think that in position and power and a big income, he'll be validated. He thinks he will be able to point to all of that and say, "Look what *I've* accomplished! I've done it myself . . . and I feel satisfied."

Of course, for some men the worst that can happen is to succeed because once they do, they find themselves asking, "Is this it? Is this all there is? What's so meaningful about this? Is this really who I am? Is this really what life is all about?" Insecurity is a word that describes most of us men, whether we realize it or not, all through our lives.

PERFORMANCE

A third word is *performance.* An old ad for a gasoline company used to read, "It's performance that counts." Most men feel that way. As Gilder said, "Manhood at the most basic level can be validated and expressed only in action. Men must perform."[3] Likewise, the renowned anthropologist Margaret Mead wrote, "The only way men can realize themselves is through their work and so they drive themselves to achieve."[4] I think there's more to men than Mead allows; she leaves out the spiritual. But still, what she says is very true.

Men are consumed with excelling, with performance. Just look at the different books and magazines that are marketed to men as opposed to women. The ones for women deal in insight and experience: "Tips to Enhance Your Communication With Your Mate," or "Five Ways to Rekindle the Romance in Your Marriage," or "How to Fight Fair in Your Marriage." That's stuff most men would never read, but women love it. It's relationally based.

You won't find those sorts of pieces in magazines geared toward men. On the whole, we aren't particularly interested in gaining more insight into ourselves. We're interested in winning, building, conquering, and new adventures. So we read: *7 Habits of Highly Effective People. How to Be a Star at Work. In Search of Excellence. Sports Illustrated. Maxim. Field and Stream.* We gobble up the article on "How to Jog Through Death Valley." Why? We don't know why. Why isn't important. It's a way to perform. We love these kinds of books and articles because when we feel like we're excelling, we feel better about ourselves.

I laugh at how this need to perform shows up in even the simple matters in life. Take driving to a vacation in Florida, for instance. My wife, like most women, loves to drink in the experience of the trip. She prefers a leisurely pace, stopping at selected sites and shopping along the way. She also enjoys historical markers. To her the travel is part of the vacation.

But not to me! It's up at 4:30 A.M. with the goal to get there in record time! If a buddy of mine drove the same route in fifteen hours, I have to do it in fourteen hours and thirty-seven minutes! For some reason it just feels better to make a race out of it.

Sherard will say, "Oh look, Robert, there's the U.S.S. Alabama! Can't we stop?"

"No way!" I say as I press the accelerator to the floor. "We've got to get there!"

Or everybody will be crying out for a potty break, and I'll be saying, "Can't you guys hold it for just another 250 miles? We've got a record to break here!"

Then there are those moments when we get lost. I always get lost at some point on a vacation trip. Sherard will ask, "How come we can't just pull in somewhere and ask for directions?" Just like a woman, asking for insight! But for a man, asking for insight is an admission of weakness. No, I have something to prove! I have to perform. I have to be able to say that I got to wherever Florida is now, with no one's help, and in record time!

This performance orientation extends to the sexual area as well. Most women just want to know if their sex life is normal. So, they'll pick up *Reader's Digest* and read an insightful article about sexual frequency in marriage. They check the frequency figures listed to find what the average is. You know — to make sure everything is okay.

Not most men! We're not interested in *Reader's Digest* or in averages. If sexual frequency is the issue, we want the *Guinness Book of World Records!* We want to know what the *maximum* frequency for sex is. Who wants to be average? Let's go for the gold!

In area after area, most men want to win because we're performance oriented. Process is meaningless. It's results that count.

So, three words paint a graphic picture of what life is like "on the inside" for men: *identity,* which relates to our deepest need; *insecurity,* which relates to a problem we'll spend our entire lives trying to solve; and *performance,* which relates to our fundamental mindset. This is the soul of manhood. It's a wise wife who keeps these in mind for they will explain much about what is going on in her husband's life.

15

What Every Husband Needs to Succeed

One of the amenities of living in Arkansas is that I can drive to the old resort town of Hot Springs and bite down on some of the most mouth-watering barbecue known to man. Everyone in Arkansas knows about McClard's Restaurant. Others outside of Arkansas know it, too. McClard's is so famous that Willard Scott, celebrity weatherman of NBC's "Today Show," judged it "best barbecue in America"!

The thing that makes McClard's barbecue so memorable, of course, is their sauce. Like so many good cooks, the McClard family won't tell you what they put in it. That's proprietary information, as top secret as the formula to Coca-Cola. Sure, barbecue sauce is barbecue sauce. But they've got two or three secret ingredients that turn theirs into world-class red.

Likewise, some wives seem to know those "secret" feminine ingredients that are crucial to a husband's stability and satisfaction in marriage. Others don't. Yet, without these ingredients, a man's self-esteem can be easily shaken. I've witnessed that firsthand in some of the marriage counseling I've done over the years. On the other hand, the wife who wisely stirs these special ingredients into her marriage will find they give her husband energy, strength, life, and happiness.

Want to know what they are? As a man, I'll be glad to tell you. Some things are just too good to keep secret!

ADMIRATION

Admiration is the first important ingredient. Every man needs a wife who will *admire* him. Remember the famous fairy tale "Snow White"? The wicked stepmother asked, as she peered into her looking glass, "Mirror, mirror on the wall, who's the fairest of them all?"

A man has two significant mirrors in his life: one is his work, the other is his wife. Looking into them, he asks important questions of identity, worth, and meaning. Both will reflect back to him strong messages about his manhood. Over time, what he receives from them will spell the difference between a life of satisfaction and a life of deep frustration.

Of the two, you as a woman are the more important over a lifetime in helping your man feel good about himself. Why? Because there are times when his work is just work. And there will be a time when he has no work. But he'll want you to be there, energizing and stabilizing his life. You are his most valuable mirror! How you feel about him, how you look at him, how you smile at him and draw alongside of him—and tell him in all sincerity, "I think you're the greatest!"—those intense feelings of admiration and respect will resurface as feelings he has for himself later.

Each time I'm involved in premarital counseling with a couple, I make sure we work through Ephesians 5 together. As we overview the passage, one of the questions I always ask the young lady is, "Are you surprised by anything Paul didn't say to you that you would have expected him to say?"

On a few occasions a woman will remark, "He doesn't tell me to love my husband, only to respect him."

Then, I'll say, "There is great wisdom there, so don't miss it."

The Scripture rarely exhorts you as a woman to love your husband. Why? It's not because he doesn't need it. He does. But there is something he needs more deeply than love. He needs your respect, your admiration. Every husband yearns for the respect of his wife. He desperately wants to know you think he is important, that he has value, and that his life on this planet is worth something. If his wife fails to give him this, inside he will feel a deep sense of loss.

My wife longs to hear me say "I love you." I say it often because I know it means so much to her. It does to every woman. But the phrase that has comparable value to me from her is not "I love you," but "I'm proud of you." Admiration is a special ingredient to your husband's happiness. Let him know what you genuinely admire about him.

SUPPORT

That brings us to a second "secret" ingredient: *support.* We're not talking about financial support here, but a crucial kind of personal and emotional support. Every man needs to know his wife stands with him. Proverbs 31:10-12 says,

> *An excellent wife, who can find?*
> *For her worth is far above jewels.*
> *The heart of her husband* trusts *in her,*
> *And he will have no lack of gain.*
> *She does him good and not evil*
> *All the days of her life.*

Can you hear the support in that? If you want to be an "excellent wife," the sort of wife that Scripture praises, you'll want to encourage your husband. You'll want to be his most loyal supporter. You'll cheer for him, back him, and inspire him to new heights! He will have no doubt you believe in him. That's what these verses are saying. In addition, I believe your man will especially need your support in three practical areas.

Support His Work

First, your husband needs your support *for* his work. How *you* feel about his work is vitally important. Work is one way he has of defining himself. So how you feel about his work translates in his mind into how you feel about him. If you encourage and back him in his work, your support stabilizes and energizes him.

But suppose you care little about what he does for a living; suppose you make no effort to even understand it; suppose you're interested only in what kind of money he makes; suppose you choose not to understand the pressure he's under; suppose you resent his work, or maybe even compete with him through your own career. Through any of these attitudes, you'll knock the props out from under your husband, and stir up his insecurity. You'll leave him feeling empty, resentful, and confused.

In his mammoth work *Seasons of a Man's Life,* Daniel Levinson found that men choose women to marry who they think will "nourish their life's vision" and help them fulfill their identity in a life work.[1] They desire wives who are behind them, encouraging them, supporting them, and cheering for them. If, after marriage, a wife fails to share in her husband's vision or participate in it, or if she becomes apathetic toward his work, or even resentful of it, then that marriage will fall into deep trouble within a surprisingly short time.

For the record, I'm not saying that as a wife you should endorse your husband's workaholism. That's an unhealthy pattern, and I would never encourage a woman to enable that. But I want you to understand how important work is to the heart and soul of your man. How you stand behind his life's work is critical to his self-esteem.

Support Him in Public

A second place he needs your support is *in public.* Have you ever seen a woman correct her husband in public, or squabble with him, or challenge him, or ridicule him? Have you ever seen a woman roll her eyes in exasperation or boredom as her husband excitedly shares his interests or dreams with friends? In such moments, she betrays him at a depth she may not understand. Public embarrassment cuts a man's ego to the quick. It ignites in him deep resentment. He may not say anything in those moments, but that doesn't mean he isn't taking note. You can read it in his face. Few things wound him more than this kind of humiliation. He rarely forgets it either. In fact, he may even seek revenge for it later. Proverbs 12:4 sums it up well:

> *An excellent wife is the crown of her husband*
> *But she who shames him is as rottenness in his bones.*

There's a story about just such an incident in the book of Esther. The Persian king, Ahasuerus, threw a lavish banquet to show off his wealth and possessions to a party of international delegates. At the height of the evening, he called for his wife, Queen Vashti. He was extremely proud of her and desired to display her beauty to all. The crowd waited for her to appear, but she didn't arrive. Embarrassed and humiliated before his friends, the king sent courtiers to fetch her. But still she refused to come.

Esther 1:12 tells the rest: "Then the king became very angry and his wrath burned within him." So it is within many a man who is shamed and embarrassed publicly—even in little ways—by the person who should be his most loyal fan. If this lack of support is chronic, he may feel so hurt and angry that he considers looking elsewhere for support. He may even do what King Ahasuerus eventually did—find another woman (Esther 2:17)!

Certainly there *is* room in every marriage for a wife to challenge her husband and point out deficiencies and problems. But not in public. The correct place is private conversation. In public, a man needs his wife's support.

Support Through the Seasons of Life

A third area in which your husband needs your support is *in the transitions of life*. As men grow older they pass through various stages, each one demanding something a bit different. A wise woman will recognize these stages and respond to her husband's needs appropriately.

For instance, if your man is in his twenties, he's trying to figure out what he's going to do in life. He's looking for a job to establish himself. In fact, he may go through a number of jobs, experimenting and learning what his capacities are. Because he's young and inexperienced, he's likely to have a lot of self-doubts and fears. As his wife, you can be a tremendous support to him, encouraging him, believing in him, giving him room to grow and even to fail. You can be an island of stability in an ocean of unknowns.

When your man reaches his thirties, you may find that he

wants to take significant risks. He's beginning to feel his confidence. Maybe he wants to get out from under his mentor or his employer, with the attitude, "I can do it better on my own!" Naturally, this desire for independence creates a lot of risk, which can be very hard on you as a woman, because you probably would prefer security at that point. You don't want him to give up a guaranteed paycheck. Yet would you want to keep this security at the cost of your husband's soul shriveling? I'm not saying that you should quietly go along with every wild-eyed scheme he cooks up! But he does need your support and understanding of his need to make a mark in the world.

In his forties your man will likely hit that middle-aged crisis of wondering whether his life counts for anything. Even if he's achieved some success, he might say, "So what? Is this important? Does it really matter? What's next? Where do I go from here?" These are good questions for him to ask. But in sorting them out, he needs someone special to talk to about the tremendous feelings of doubt and fear and insecurity they stir up. He especially needs a sensitive wife who can help lend perspective to his accomplishments and what he's done right. You, more than any other person, can build him up during a period of great instability.

Eventually a man reaches his sixties. He retires and gives up the center stage of power he's held for so long. Naturally, he asks, "What value do I have now?" A supportive wife is a man's best friend during this critical time. During this last phase of life, he needs to discover a new purpose, a new direction for his final years. How does he get that? I believe his best hope for insight lies with you—the wife he has come to trust in because you do "him good and not evil all the days of his life." Wives, never ever underestimate the power of your personal support. It's what every husband needs to succeed.

There are, of course, two additional ingredients every wise wife will mix into her marriage. We'll cover these in the next chapter.

16

What Else a Husband Needs to Succeed

COMPANIONSHIP

There's a third powerful ingredient that can help your husband become the leader God wants him to be, and that's for you as his wife to *become his companion*. Unfortunately, many couples lose touch with one another as far as the simple pleasure of enjoying one another's company goes. Husband and wife, yes; friends, no. They allow their marriage to succumb to that "creeping separateness" I mentioned in chapter 4. Over time they gradually drift apart. They forget the fun of experiencing life together. So, they build separate worlds that have little in common. Yet, Solomon said,

> Two are better than one because they have a good return for their labor. For if either of them falls, the one will lift up his companion. But woe to the one who falls when there is not another to lift him up. Furthermore, if two lie down together they keep warm, but how can one be warm alone? (Ecclesiastes 4:9-11)

I love this passage because it expresses the companionship marriage was meant to give. It speaks of the wisdom and warmth of two people staying close.

Sharing Interests

In marriage, a husband needs a wife who will share *his interests.* Unfortunately, it is easy for a wife to lose sight of this need in the hustle of running a home, having children, or pursuing her own career. She can quickly lose interest in ball games, fishing, sports, and hobbies that at one time she shared with him.

For a busy wife, this might not seem like a big problem. Besides, her husband probably hasn't complained. Even without her, he continues his jogging, his fishing, his going to ball games. So, what's the big deal? The deal is the companionship *has stopped!* This may come as a surprise to most women, but your involvement in the things he loves is extremely important to your husband. He loves to have you with him. He may not articulate it very often, but the need is certainly there.

Willard Harley pointed out in his book *His Needs, Her Needs* that "spending recreational time with his wife is second only to sex [in importance] for the typical husband."[1] Harley reached this conclusion after interviewing thousands of couples about their real needs.

It may be a well-kept secret to some, but ladies, your husband wants you to "come along with him" and share in his interests.

Marriage Is for Dreamers

Your husband also needs a companion to share in his dreams. You heard right—his dreams. Men spend a tremendous amount of energy making sure they are doing what they need to be doing, and what they want to be doing! It's that insecurity issue again. A man needs constant reassurance he's in the right place, doing the right thing. It's energizing to him to be able to test himself by dreaming out loud. That's where you, his companion in life, come in. You are the trusted soul-mate he can dream out loud *with!* But let me warn you, wives, when your husband is dreaming, he can sound off the wall!

One woman expressed it this way: "My husband is nuts! He sits around after supper and talks about how we should pick up and move to Alaska! If we both work, we'll have a real stake in about five or six years, he says. We'll spend all night talking about it and figuring out how we would do it. Will he go up there first and look for a job and a place to live? Or should we both go and hope for the best?

"A week later, he'll be sitting around talking about how he ought to take a couple of courses at the university toward his master's degree. It would make a big difference in his chances for getting ahead, he says.

"It seems to me he comes home with a different crazy scheme every week. I used to take him seriously, but now I know it's all talk. What do you do with a man like that?"

Does your husband dream with you? I do that with Sherard all the time. There are frequent occasions when I get so confused and frustrated with my work that I wonder, "Is this the right vocation for me? What am I doing here?" In that emotional state, I need someone to pour my heart out to, someone to help me reevaluate, and consider new possibilities and options. Maybe I should be a coach . . . or a consultant . . . or . . .

My wife has faithfully weathered many hours of those kinds of discussions. I'm sure some of the things I've said have scared her to death. At times, she probably felt like saying, "Well, that's the craziest thing I've ever heard! You can't coach!" Or, "You can't change now—not after all we've been through!" Or, "We can't do that! We'd lose the house!" Unfortunately, those kinds of responses may cause a man to hold back from expressing his dreams to his wife.

A *wise* woman, on the other hand, is patient with her husband during dream sessions. She understands that after three or four weeks of getting pushed around at his job, it's only natural for him to start dreaming about becoming a professional mountain climber or joining a circus or some other crazy scheme. She also realizes that dreaming is his way of evaluating. Often, he's really asking: Is what I'm doing *valuable?* Am I any good? Does my life count for anything? Is there anything else I could do? What do you think of me? (P.S.: I'm feeling insecure!) Questions like these are the very reason you as a wife need to be there, sharing his dreams.

Sherard seizes these moments of apprehension and insecurity and says to me, "Robert, tell me why you want to change careers.

Why a ranch in Wyoming? I want to know how you feel." Then she often tells me again that I'm doing well where I am. Even when I come up with some really wild concoctions, she doesn't panic. She often draws up close and says, "If you want to do it, I'm open because I know you'll take care of us. I'll follow you. You're a good man." Wow! Let me tell you, when she finishes that kind of affirmation, my whole identity has changed! I feel reaffirmed as a man!

Men dream like that all the way through life. And more often than not, they're only seeking redefinition and affirmation, not a real job change. So, ladies, relax — and give him your ear. Affirm him. Share his dreams and his interests. In marriage, *two are always better than one.*

PHYSICAL RESPONSIVENESS

A fourth and final way that you as a wife can help your husband is *by your response to him physically.* Few things affirm a man in his masculinity as does his wife's sexual responsiveness. Spontaneous hugs, kisses, and other demonstrations of affection, as well as intercourse, do more than make a man feel good. These actions meet a much deeper need. They reassure a man. They confirm him in his masculinity!

A major mistake that a wife should be sure to avoid is assuming that in sex, all a man wants to do is please himself. A wife who carries that kind of unhealthy perspective can make a man feel cheap, dirty, even ugly inside. Men are intensely physical creatures. God has designed us that way. But ladies, that doesn't mean that all your husband wants is your body, or just a mere moment of ecstasy. No, there is something more than this that makes intercourse special to him.

In the book *His Needs, Her Needs,* Willard Harley wrote,

> When a man chooses a wife, he promises to remain faithful to her for life. This means that he believes his wife will be his only sexual partner "until death do us part." He makes this commitment because he trusts her to be as sexually interested in him as he is in her.[2]

Sexually interested—I wish I could burn those words into the soul of every wife. It's what makes a man feel like a man! A husband doesn't want a body to perform on, he wants a person who will respond to him in the physical terms that are so meaningful to him. Husbands aren't any more excited about "have to" sex than a wife is in hearing "I love you" from a husband she feels is "having to." It's the "want to" that is so important. Without it, a husband loses a sense of his masculine self-esteem.

Women, let me tell you a very special secret about men and sex. This is something most husbands will never, ever tell their wives, but they are thinking it. In one way or another, they are thinking it all the time. A man is seeking to know two important things about himself from his wife in intercourse (remember, you are his mirror). He's asking two important questions that are deeply linked to his identity, the insecurity he feels, and his performance make-up. The first is, "Can I perform as a man?" We're not talking about his having an orgasm, we're talking about performance. "Am I performing well? Because of how I perform sexually, *do you feel drawn to me?*"

The second question is, "Do I give my wife pleasure?" This question is crucial. The most important thing to a man in sex is how his wife enjoys his lovemaking. Real sexual fulfillment for a husband ultimately does *not* come from the pleasure he receives, but *from the pleasure he senses you, his wife, receive from him!* This truth is a total surprise to some women. But it is the truth, trust me.

For a man, the most powerful moments in sex are those that answer these two critical questions, reaffirming his masculinity. His orgasm can't answer those questions. Only *you,* his wife, can answer those questions! That's why your response is so vital. If you want your husband to leave your bedside saying "Yessss!" inside, then let him know you enjoy being with him. Respond to his lovemaking. Let him know how he's doing. Talk to him. Say, "That feels so good!" or "You're terrific!" or "I can't wait to be with you again!" Your response will have more impact on completing and affirming his manhood than *any* physical pleasure he receives. Remember, a man is looking for confirmation of his masculine identity in his wife's responsiveness.

On the other hand, a wife who gives in to her husband's advances with an "I'll let him have what he wants" attitude deeply frustrates him. He will pick up on it easily, and it will stir up more insecurity than pleasure. He'll come away feeling empty and having questions about himself.

A wise wife makes sure her husband has *no doubt* about his manhood when he leaves her bedside.

ADVANCED STUDIES IN YOUR MAN

Admiration, support, companionship, and physical responsiveness. These four ingredients go a long way toward "completing" your husband. If you follow these suggestions, I believe you're well on your way toward a level of insight and intimacy with your husband that few wives ever achieve. But perhaps some of you will want to go even further. Maybe you want to get a Ph.D. in your husband, to really go for the gold and know him inside out. If so, here are two steps, two "advanced courses," you can take.

First, *become a student of the man in your life.* Observe him. I would even suggest writing your observations down to help you more accurately pay attention to him. Is he the kind who comes home and wants things to be neat? Does neatness affect his moods? Write it down. Is he the kind who gets up on Saturday and has to mow three or four lawns to feel good about himself? When does he get depressed? What usually comes before that depression? When is he most happy? Write it down. Always be on the lookout for clues that your husband gives you about what makes him tick. In time, these observations will fall into definite patterns that will allow you, "the expert," to respond to him more wisely and appropriately.

Second, *broaden your knowledge base.* There are so many books and resources available to help you do that. I've already mentioned *His Needs, Her Needs* by Willard Harley. It's an excellent start. Another book I recommend is *The Art of Understanding Your Mate* by Cecil Osborne. He has included case studies that illustrate situations you find in your own marriage. A more challenging study is George Gilder's *Men and Marriage.* It takes an in-depth look at what makes men men, and shows how women

are the most powerful influence on the ability of men to live productive, meaningful lives. Dr. Joyce Brothers has written *What
Every Woman Should Know About Men.* I don't agree with everything she says, but the section on sex is helpful.

If your husband is struggling with identity, *Men in Mid-Life
Crisis* by Jim Conway might be helpful. And my friends Dennis and
Barbara Rainey have written *Building Your Mate's Self Esteem,*
which has outstanding insights and practical suggestions for women
about relating to their husbands.

There are, of course, many, many others. A Christian bookstore
will have a host of titles to show you. But these would make a great
start for any wife who is serious about really helping and loving her
husband. So, go for it!

FOR DISCUSSION

1. Reread the first few paragraphs of chapter 13. How have you
   experienced these differences (in the ways men's and women's
   brains function) in your marriage. Give each other some examples. How can knowing this difference help you understand each
   other? How will you use this information to communicate more
   effectively?
2. Husbands, take a few minutes alone to think through how you
   could change the ways or times you talk with your wife. Ask her
   if you're thinking in the right direction.

   Wives, take a few minutes alone to think through how you
   could change the ways and times you talk with your husband. Ask
   him if you're thinking in the right direction. Discuss your individual answers together.
3. This section used several key words to describe what husbands
   need to succeed in marriage. Define each of these terms in your
   own words: admiration, support, companionship, physical responsiveness.
4. Wives, think of one way you can show your husband that you are
   committed to helping him feel secure in his identity and in your
   relationship. What one way can you demonstrate that you admire
   his skills as a husband and parent? Remembering that he thinks

concretely, how can you make sure he knows you support him, no matter what? Finally, think through the times he's responded positively to your touch, times he's most enjoyed your sexual relationship. Can you multiply those positive responses by increasing the frequency of those touches?

Husbands, think through these same questions: How can your wife express her admiration for you? How can she demonstrate her support for you—even for some of your crazy ideas? How can she make it clear that she's committed for the long haul—your whole life together—as your companion? How can she increase your physical intimacy, both in sexual and nonsexual ways?

Now discuss these questions. It will probably seem awkward, but think of the results of starting to carry out some of these things!

5. Reread the section "Support Through the Seasons of Life" at the end of chapter 15. Discuss where your husband is right now. With that in mind, what are his greatest needs? Wives, how can you help provide for these needs?

Part Six

RESPONSES THAT ENERGIZE THE ROLES

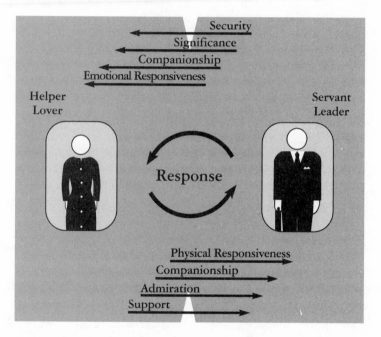

17
The "S" Word

No word brings more winces and grimaces to a discussion on marriage than the "S" word, *submission.* The word sounds downright demeaning, especially to North American ears. It comes off as an archaic expression from the days of slaves and second-class citizens, a code word for "barefoot and pregnant." After twenty-five or more years of feminist activism, any teacher who says that wives should be "submissive" to their husbands is liable to touch off a firestorm of controversy.

Yet the Bible uses the term.[1] Furthermore, submission is presented in almost every biblical example as an act of honor. For instance, in Ephesians 5:22-24 (NIV), Paul likens a wife's submission to her husband to the Church's submission to Christ:

> Wives, submit to your husbands as to the Lord. For the husband is the head of the wife as Christ is the head of the Church, his body, of which he is the Savior. Now as the church submits to Christ, so also wives should submit to their husbands in everything.

I have yet to hear a sermon or read a book that decries a believer's submission to Christ as something negative, abusive, or chauvinistic. Yet that's exactly what has happened to the idea of wives submitting to their husbands. Clearly, something is wrong. I believe we've lost sight of what submission really means. Therefore, let me offer three statements to help achieve a proper understanding of this important concept.

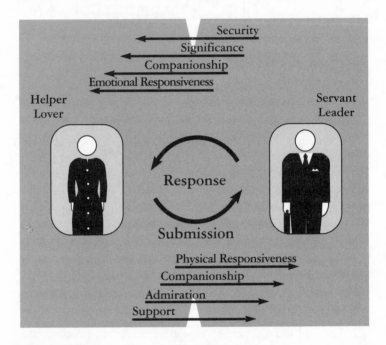

Biblical Submission Is a Christlike Response to Recognized Leadership

Whenever the Bible instructs someone to submit or "subject," an authority or a designated leader is in view. A common pattern, for instance, can be found in 1 Peter 2:13, where Peter tells believers, "Submit yourselves for the Lord's sake to every human institution." He's talking about authority structures, and he lists some of them: government officials and believers at large (2:13-17); slave-owners and slaves (2:18-25); husbands and wives (3:1-7).[2] The New Testament recognizes clear-cut lines of authority and leadership, and tells Christians to "submit" as Christ would to those authorities — that is, to recognize and respond to that leadership.

Notice that *all* believers are called to submit to various authorities. It's a part of their ultimate submission to Jesus Christ as Lord. In fact, whenever the New Testament talks about submission, it links the authority figure to Christ. For instance, Peter says "submit yourselves *for the Lord's sake* (emphasis added)." Whenever we as believers deal with someone in authority, we are to respond as if Christ Himself were leading us.

Such submission involves both attitude and action. For instance, in the marriage relationship, a submissive wife's attitude would be, "God has appointed my husband to a position of leadership, and I'm going to respect him as a leader and help him do all that God wants him to do." Then she would back up that perspective with action, helping her man accomplish God's desires.

Please note: *A biblically submissive wife's focus is not on enabling wrong behavior, but on empowering her husband to pursue right behavior*—to become the man God wants him to be, and the leader God wants him to be. That's an extremely important point. God never asks a wife (or any believer) to do what is wrong. After all, she ultimately serves Christ, and He never asks us to do wrong.

One woman came to a counselor after her husband was arrested for sexual assault on a minor. Needless to say, she felt devastated. At the counselor's request, she related the history of her marriage. For years her husband had immersed himself in pornography, even though both of them were Christians. The first time she saw him with such material, she was too shocked to say anything. They were newlyweds, and she was afraid to think he might have a problem.

Finally she asked him about it one day. He replied, "This is just something men do; it's normal." That didn't sound right to her, but she was too ashamed to mention it to anyone else. She was also new in town and didn't have any close friends yet. Nor did she feel comfortable approaching her minister about such a delicate matter.

One day her husband brought home a videotape showing graphic scenes of sexual intercourse. He played it on their television and then began making love to his wife. When she recoiled in disgust, he became extremely angry, shouting, "What's the matter with you?! You're my wife! We're supposed to have sex together!"

"But, honey," she said, "I don't think it's right to watch that sort of thing while we're making love. It makes me feel dirty."

"Look, there's nothing dirty about sex!" he replied. "Anyway, I like to have that on when you and I have sex. And since I'm the husband, that's the way it's going to be. Remember when we got married, you said you were going to submit to me? Well, here's a chance to submit!"

Stunned, the woman went along with this scheme. In time, her husband began bringing home tapes that were not only sexual but violent as well. He also talked her into engaging in various forms of sex that she found weird and degrading. So she really wasn't surprised when the police showed up at her door to say that he had been arrested.

I feel sorry for this woman. Without question, her husband was a sick man who needed help. But she made a terrible mistake in accepting his argument that it was her duty to go against her convictions and engage in sick sex with him. Behavior of that sort has nothing to do with biblical submission.

Submission Is Not the Woman's Role in Marriage

For years I thought it was. Like most of us, I was taught that the role of the husband was to be the leader and the role of the wife was to submit. The husband was to be assertive, active, aggressive, and creative. The wife was to be more or less compliant, passively going along with her husband's direction. Over time, I began to see what a tremendous error that was.

As we've already discussed, a wife's role is that of being a "helper" and a "lover." Her role is filled with all kinds of initiative and creativity. So where does that leave submission? I believe submission is not a role *at all*, not in the technical sense. A better definition would be to describe it more as a *response* than a role.

In part 4, we discussed at length the wife's role in marriage. I hope you observed that submission was not mentioned. *Submission is a wife's response to her husband's role*—a response that frees him to carry out his role of servant-leadership. That's an important distinction. It's not just a case of semantics.

Take another look at Ephesians 5. This passage is probably cited more than any other when arguing for the wife's "role of submission." Yet, I argue that this passage is primarily a text on the husband's role, not the wife's. It urges him to be a Christlike servant and leader to his wife. It tells him how. The intermittent exhortations on submission are not intended to be seen as the wife's role (her essential function as designed by God), but only as a Christlike *response* that affirms her husband's role, while encouraging him to lead.

Let me illustrate. Every election day I go to a polling booth and help elect government leaders. When someone wins the election, he assumes a role of leadership. His role, the fundamental purpose for which he has been elected, is to govern, to represent me and the rest of the citizenry in making the necessary decisions to sustain our community.

What is my *role* as a citizen? Is it to obey the law and pay taxes? No! If that's all my citizenship means, I won't have any income. I won't be able to pay my taxes. Obeying laws and paying taxes is not my fundamental *role;* those things are my *response* to the government's role. I do those things as a way of supporting and upholding the government I help elect. But as a citizen my primary *role* is something different—namely, to pursue my vocation, raise my family, and make a personal contribution to others in my society.

If the only thing that citizenship in this country meant was to obey the law and pay taxes, I don't think people would be clamoring to immigrate to this country. I think there would be a mass exodus—or, more likely, mass revolt! In the same way, if the only thing that Christian marriage meant for women was submission, if that were their primary role, then I wouldn't blame them if they rejected Christian marriage.

However, submission is not a role but a response—a very special, empowering response. Properly understood and practiced, it affirms and energizes a husband's leadership in the home and releases him to lead. Therefore . . .

The Wife's Response of Submission Helps Her Husband Fulfill His God-Given Role

God wants every husband to lead his family with Christlike service and leadership. But the odds are against most men ever becoming servant-leaders. That's a sobering reality, and it should be a warning to every wife. It's not that men can't lead, or don't want to. But so much is stacked against them from the very start.

First of all, *the world system is against us.* It seems that everything we watch or read or hear pulls us in the direction of being "lords," not servant-leaders. I can't fully express what a powerful influence that is!

For instance, on Friday afternoon a man will be talking with his buddies about the weekend. They'll get all excited about what a great time they could have on the golf course on Saturday. Never mind that most of them will have to forsake responsibilities at home! It's nearly impossible for many men to decline an invitation to tee off with the other guys, just so they can fulfill prior commitments to their wife and kids. We know we should. But the peer pressure is unbelievable. It's as if our masculinity is on the line!

Furthermore, *a man's own flesh is against him.* We saw in Genesis 3:16 what a man's flesh is inclined to do as a result of the Fall—to oppress, dominate, and rule over women. A man's flesh encourages him to do that every day. It can start as soon as he gets out of bed. His wife runs around the house getting the kids and herself ready for the day, and what does he do? He sits calmly and quietly, enjoying his coffee, reading the paper, taking a shower, having breakfast. He ignores any sense of responsibility to help. And if his wife complains, well, that's a terrible imposition and he makes life so difficult that she just backs off and never asks for his help again.

The world and the flesh—that's two strikes! Number three is a curve ball: Sometimes a man's own wife is against him. If she resists and competes with him and criticizes him, I don't think there's much chance of him ever leading in a godly way. Most husbands will not respond to competition with anything resembling servant-leadership. It's just too much. Most men will retreat from their high and holy calling and start concentrating on themselves and their own desires. They'll shrug off their leadership responsibilities and move on.

That's where the game is really lost. So often when the husband retreats from his role like that, the wife will respond by taking charge. "If he won't lead, I will!" But let me tell you, it's the worst thing a woman can do.

If she competes with him, or criticizes him, or constantly corrects whatever efforts he does make, or steps in to take over when he fails, I don't think she can expect him to hang in there because he won't. She can expect him to withdraw—not to physically leave the home necessarily, but to spiritually, psychologically, and emotionally withdraw. He'll find some other turf besides home in which to exercise his leadership. For him, home is a lost cause.

WHERE WOMEN LEAD

If I were to reduce all of this to a simple principle, it would be: *Where wives seek to lead, husbands leave.* Husbands will abdicate their God-given responsibility. Most won't fight their wives for leadership; they'll just turn it over and walk away. Everything in the culture encourages them to do that. Everything in their sinful nature encourages them to do that. If their own wives start fighting them for control, then they'll quickly abdicate.

As a wife, can you see where the biblical concept of submission comes into play in your relationship? The reality of marriage is that your husband has been given an awesome responsibility, a job that, quite frankly, is beyond him. He needs help to pull it off. He needs God's help. But he also needs your help as his wife. He needs a *biblically* "submissive" wife, one who recognizes his leadership and whose daily responses empower him to lead.

Submission is a way of telling your husband, "I believe in you! I'm with you! You can do it!" It's a way of keeping him the leader, even when he doesn't want to be the leader anymore. You're helping him become what God wants him to become. As he struggles, as he attempts—sometimes feebly and sometimes boldly—to give structure and clarity and direction to your family, submission is a way of validating his role. By it you say, "You're the servant-leader here, and I'm behind you all the way!" What a healthy *response!*

A simple illustration may be helpful at this point. When Sherard and I approach a door, my wife will usually stop and wait for me to open it. It's not that she is incapable of opening it for herself. Quite the contrary, she is very capable. But in waiting on and deferring to me, she is communicating a strong message of my responsibility in one relationship we have agreed on. Her action declares in that moment what I have been called to do (whether I feel like it or not) and what she will *not* do.

Though this is only a symbolic gesture, this same attitude extends to more serious responsibilities I have assumed in our marriage, such as providing for our family, paying bills, prayer, giving direction to the family, and so on. Again, it is not that my wife is incapable of assuming responsibility for these things. She is capable. In fact, in a number of homes the wife may actually be more capable. But in refusing to take charge or control, a wife is reinforcing her husband's leadership role rather than robbing him of it. Her submission gently but clearly reaffirms what he has agreed to do and what she has agreed not to do. In the end, submission helps a man become a responsible husband and leader.

I also can tell you from personal experience that for the man who is trying to lead, a wife's submission is a wonderful and affirming response. It fills him with confidence and a belief that he really can love his wife as Christ loved the Church. But if his best efforts—or even worse, his failures—are met with resistance, rebuke, and reprisals, then he'll more than likely revert to the selfish, lording chauvinist that lurks in his sinful flesh—the character that God said would be there after the Fall.

Husbands, God has called you to lead your family in the same way that Christ leads His Church. He wants you to love your wife, to care for her as you would yourself. That will take every ounce of courage, strength, and determination you have. Even then, you'll need God's enabling to succeed. You'll also need your wife's submission. You cannot demand that she "submit" to you. Not at all. Though Scripture urges her to submit to your leadership, it never once authorizes you to give her that command yourself. Submission is her choice, her willful response, and frankly, her privilege. It's between her and God. Your focus needs to be on your servant-leadership, not on her submission. That is your biblically assigned role in marriage.

Wives, as your husband seeks to carry out his role, you have a choice to make. You can battle him for control or you can *help* him by affirming his leadership with this godly response. God asks you to "submit" to his leadership, a *response* that frees him to carry out his role.

18

The Masculine Counterpart
to the "S" Word

One of the most important principles in this book is that submission is not a woman's role in marriage. Rather, it is a *response* of affirmation a wife gives to her husband as he seeks to carry out his *role* of servant-leadership. It is a response that frees him to be more effective in fulfilling his tremendous leadership responsibility. Meanwhile, a wife carries a tremendous responsibility of her own in her role as helper, which includes being a husband-lover and a child-lover.

That leads us to ask a very important question: Does the husband have a similar *response* of affirmation that energizes his wife's role? The answer is an emphatic "Yes!" (although it's rarely talked about). In Scripture, there is a masculine counterpart to the "S" word *submission:* the "P" word—*praise!* If you're a husband, you need to understand the power and importance of praise as a *response* to the role your wife plays in your marriage. Just as her submission frees and empowers you to carry out your core role, so your praise frees and empowers your wife to carry out her core role. Both responses are life-giving to your marriage.

A wife needs and deserves praise—and a lot of it. She should constantly receive honor and affirmation from you for the "husband-loving" and "child-loving" support that she imparts. No one can really see that nurture the way you, her husband, can. And you had better constantly tell your wife how important she is, how significant is her awesome power of being there for you and your children. If not, she will likely feel the way too many woman feel—that her support is either not needed or not important. We know that nothing could be further from the truth.

Yet psychologist James Dobson, in his book *What Wives Wish Their Husbands Knew About Women,* pointed out that the most pressing and troubling problem among women today is low self-esteem.[1] They just don't feel good about themselves. They don't feel deeply that what they do really counts or has value, even though it does. Why? What's the problem? Could it be that someone special to them has forgotten to tell them that they are appreciated and that their contributions are vital? Is that the case in your home?

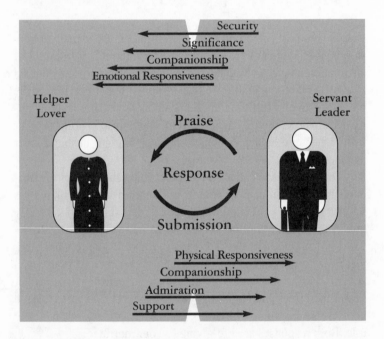

PRAISE WITH A CAPITAL "P"
Certainly a lack of submission can undercut any man's attempts at leadership. But I hardly think submission has much to do with

many of the problems in marriage today. I think far more could be accomplished by helping men understand how critical their response of praise is to healthy marriages and happy wives.

We see that challenge in 1 Peter 3:7, where Peter tells husbands to "grant her [your wife] honor as a fellow heir of the grace of life." That is, treat her with respect and dignity. Let her enjoy all the benefits, rights, and comforts that you enjoy. Nurture, encourage, and praise her as a person with thoughts, feelings, and volition. Place her right beside you, equal in value and importance. Stand by her, and remind her that apart from her, you and your family could not make it—not well. She is the critical difference!

The husband of the woman in Proverbs 31 evidently had this kind of insight. Proverbs 31 urges a wife to fear the Lord more than she fears her culture. That godly fear has many positive implications for her family. It has implications for her as well. She is often pulled out of the spotlight with her real work out of sight. How does a woman survive? By constantly being reminded of how important she is and being honored by those who receive the benefits of her service—service that no one else sees. Notice the praise the Proverbs 31 wife receives from her husband and children (verses 28-30):

Her children rise up and bless her;
Her husband also, and he praises her, saying:
"Many daughters have done nobly,
But you excel them all."
Charm is deceitful and beauty is vain,
But a woman who fears the Lord, she shall be praised.

That's Praise with a capital "P"! No other response brings feelings of honor and deep satisfaction to a woman in quite the same way.

One Mother's Day I gave Sherard expensive perfume along with a card. At the bottom of the card I had written a brief note. It was interesting to watch the various responses that followed. She opened the present and that was fine. She smiled and said thanks. And she appreciated the card itself. But I could see her eyes quickly drop down to the little message I'd written at the bottom. It said, "Sherard, I am so honored that you would pick me to love. You make coming home the best part of the day for all of us!" Suddenly, for that moment, through a very simple, brief statement, her countenance took on a completely different look. It was the look of a satisfied woman. She realized, again, that her sacrificial, self-effacing efforts to be a godly wife were worth it. They were appreciated. *She* was appreciated, valued, honored.

SO TELL ME WHAT TO DO!

Now I can guess what some of you husbands are thinking at this point. Because men tend to be so task-oriented, you're probably mumbling something like this: "Okay, Robert wants me to buy a card and write a nice 'touchy-feely' note on it and give it to my wife so she'll feel appreciated." Right? "Just give me the bottom line, Robert. Tell me what I have to do. Give me a task. Send her flowers? Buy her candy? Give her a day at the shopping mall? Hug her and tell her I love her? What is it?"

Certainly those things have their place, and I encourage you to make your praise tangible through special moments and special gifts. But those things, as cherished as they are, can't replace an even more valuable way of exalting your wife. She needs your praise *most* on an *everyday basis!* Without an everyday form of praise and honor, special moments can ring hollow — maybe even a bit manipulative. But when it's present every day, then it's obvious you really do mean it.

So how can you sing your wife's praises on an everyday basis? *How* can you honor her as one who is a co-heir in your marriage? Let's look again at the Ephesians 5 passage. Earlier, in regard to your core role as a husband, we said that you should be a servant-leader in your home as Christ is to the Church (verses - 28-30, NIV):

In this same way, husbands ought to love their wives as their own bodies. He who loves his wife loves himself. After all, no one ever hated his own body, but he feeds and cares for it, just as Christ does the church — for we are members of his body.

This passage offers two specific ways a man can honor and praise his wife in the day-to-day living of married life.

EQUAL TREATMENT — THE EVERYDAY WAY TO HONOR

Imagine a human being whose self-interest ends from the neck down; in other words, only the head matters. Whatever the head wants, the head gets. If the head wants a shampoo and a shave, it gets that. If the head wants a pair of $235 sunglasses, it gets them. If the head wants a massage, it gets one. The head is pampered and primped and, quite frankly, puffed up!

But, oh, the rest of the body! From the neck down things are in sad shape. The body is bloated and flabby because it never gets the exercise it needs. It smells to high heaven, and sores and infections have broken out, because it never gets a bath. The body bears scars from where cuts and scrapes were never attended to. Its fingernails and toenails are dirty and uneven, obviously ignored. In short, the body shows every sign of neglect and mistreatment, to the point of abuse.

Would you want a body like that? Of course not! As Paul says, "No one ever hated his own body." No healthy individual lives from the head up. Yet the man who fails to love his wife does exactly that. He treats himself one way, but his wife completely differently.

Ephesians 5 says that Christlike love means treating your wife with the same respect and concern and care as you give yourself. That little word "as" in verse 28 acts like an equal sign. To love your wife *as* your own body means treating her *equally.*

It does *not* mean treating her like a man! You don't buy her the health club membership or the fishing rod or the license at the duck club that you might get for yourself (unless, of course, she would appreciate those things). But neither does it mean that you buy yourself those things and leave her to sit at home bored to tears.

So what does equal treatment look like? You might start by comparing the vehicle you drive to the one she drives. How about the time you have to yourself versus the time she has to herself? What memberships is she able to enjoy? What hobbies is she able to pursue? How much money is budgeted for her personal use, as compared to yours? How much time does she have to be with her friends when measured against the time you are with your friends? What opinions is she free to express and what causes is she free to support? What kind of language are your children allowed to use with her? How are the in-laws and your friends permitted to treat her? What limits are placed on the amount of stress she has to put up with? What preference is given to her tastes in music, art, films, sports, decorating, furniture, vacations, food, even pets? How would the commendation she receives for her work stack up against the recognition and awards you receive for your work?

Many other issues could be mentioned. The point is that so often a husband will order the family in terms of his priorities and preferences, but neglect his wife completely. In a very real way, he treats her like a second-class citizen. That's giving her the *unequal* treatment. And no extravagant material gift for a birthday or anniversary will make up for it.

CONSTANT COMMENT — THE EVERYDAY WAY TO PRAISE

Notice there's a second clue in the Ephesians 5 passage. Verse 29 (NIV) points out, "No one ever hated his own body, but he feeds and cares for it." The words *feeds and cares for* are noteworthy. In Greek they convey an ongoing activity, to *keep feeding and nourishing,* to *keep caring for.* There's an idea of constancy and regularity. Here's a second way you love your wife—*constantly.*

I don't know too many men who look in the mirror to shave and comb their hair and make sure everything is shipshape, then neglect to do that again for another forty years. Yet some men think it's normal to express their love at the wedding and then never mention it again for forty years of marriage!

That's a tragedy! A woman not only needs constant love, she needs to be told she is loved constantly. One night of celebration and affection, one note every year on your anniversary, one arrangement of flowers on her birthday are not going to cut it! Your wife needs constant, regular, daily and hourly love, attention, praise, and "I love you's." Don't get the idea that she's psychologically weak or emotionally crippled. Not at all. Rather that affirmation opens and nourishes her soul so that she grows and develops into all God intends her to be. It keeps her encouraged to keep doing what's right and best for the family.

Husbands, your wife will thrive on praise—but not on manipulation. If you try to butter her up with sweet words and kindness so you can get your own way, she'll see right through it. Even if she doesn't, that's no way to treat her. It's deceptive, it's unhealthy, and it's sin. Christlike love is not manipulation. Instead, it means treating your wife equally and constantly with the same care and concern you give yourself.

Looking over the annals of civilizations past and present, the renowned anthropologist Margaret Mead wrote, "Women are happiest, not when given position and power, but when the creative contributions of the maternal role are upheld . . . when being wife and mother are viewed as important and respectable."[2] Who honors women with that importance and respect? No one can do it like a husband. No one else's praise matters quite as much. By our everyday words and actions we must communicate to our wives that we value who they are and what they do. They have perhaps the most awesome assignment under Heaven—to "be there" for us and our children. They need to know we sincerely believe that, too!

FOR DISCUSSION

1. Define submission as you've always thought of it. Did you think of it in terms of a role in marriage? As subjection to an authority?
2. How has your definition or understanding of submission changed after reading this section? Husbands, what do you think your responsibility is to help your wife fulfill this response to your servant-leadership? Wives, answer that, too—What's your husband's responsibility? Discuss together what this response to submission might look like in everyday life.
3. Define the words *praise* and *honor* as you've always thought of them. Have you ever thought of praise as the husband's counterpart to submission? Wives, how can you help your husband fulfill this response to your role as husband-lover and child-lover? Husbands, how can your wife help you respond in this way as she fulfills her role? Discuss together what this response of praise and honor might look like in everyday life.

Part Seven
PROBLEMS AND SOLUTIONS

19

Common "Head"-Aches

In the last decade or so, talk-show host and comedian David Letterman has popularized the idea of "Top Ten Lists." Each night, his lists provide humorous—and sometimes insight-ful—glimpses into cultural issues, politics, and entertainment. The lists have been copied so much that most people think of Letterman when they hear the three words "Top Ten List."

In this chapter I have a list of my own—a list of the five worst leadership styles that men use in their homes. My "top five" picks are borne out of years of observation, study, and counseling. Some of you will probably disagree with the order of my selections. But I don't think anyone would quibble over the picks themselves. All five are distortions of the biblical concept of "headship" discussed in chapter 6. Unfortunately, there's no humor in these, either.

Christ has laid down a beautiful pattern for us as husbands in His tender yet strong leadership of His bride, the Church. Obviously, none of us lives up to that ideal perfectly. But perfec-tion is not something God expects of us. His call is for us to press forward (Philippians 3:12). As we do, our grasp of biblical head-ship becomes more and more firm, and its effect on our marriage more and more positive.

Yet, some men miss out on this wonderful truth for a variety of reasons. Whether it's due to ignorance, spiritual shallowness, emotional damage, poor modeling, or selfishness, they present to their wives a distorted image of leadership. To them, "headship" means something very different from the picture painted in Ephesians 5.

Therefore, let me introduce you to five leadership profiles that drive more wives into discouragement than any others I know. I urge every man reading this chapter: Look out for any similarities between the way you treat your wife and the patterns described here. If you find any, mark them well! Your wife is probably paying an immense price for any unhealthy behavior you identify with on the following pages. Of course, it doesn't have to stay that way. But the first step to any change is to recognize that a problem exists. So take a hard look.

Here, then, in David Letterman's "countdown" format are my "Top Five" most discouraging male-headship models.

FIVE: IRRESPONSIBLE HEADSHIP

It seems cruel to refer to anyone as "worthless," but in Brian's case the monicker fits. He is lazy, irresponsible, unreliable, and just no good; in other words, he's worthless! He's not stupid, though. He's a master at conning and manipulating others—especially his wife, Patricia—into taking responsibility for him.

Before they married, Brian made all kinds of wonderful-sounding promises. They would build a beautiful house, she would be able to finish college, and Patricia's mother would live with them in her old age. None of these dreams has materialized. Six months after the wedding, Brian was out of a job. Since then he has bounced from one get-rich-quick scheme to another, losing a lot of money in the process. Were it not for Patricia's diligent work as the office manager for a doctor's group, the couple easily would have been forced into bankruptcy.

Brian always thinks he's one step away from hitting it big. "This time I can really feel it," he loves to say when opportunity appears to be knocking. "This time I just know something big is going to happen!" Trouble is, that "something" never quite happens.

In reality, Brian is using Patricia. He's more than happy to let her make all the decisions. He even buys her flowers and gives her little gifts to show his "appreciation." (Never mind that he blew a month's paycheck on a television they didn't need. Or that he left the car windows down overnight, allowing two inches of rain to collect on the floor!)

Brian is nothing but a little boy in search of a mommy, and he seems to have found one in Patricia. He is thoroughly self-centered, but manages to appear to others as a loving and devoted husband. On her own, Patricia lacks the resolve to stand up to his slovenly ways. She lacks the personal strength to force him to grow up and take responsibility for himself. As her respect for Brian dies, the pain grows.

FOUR: EMOTIONALLY DETACHED HEADSHIP

Allen is one of the most stable and even-tempered men in his community. He has been asked to serve on the boards of numerous organizations because of his organized mind and methodical way of making decisions.

Consequently, few would imagine that Allen has troubles at home. His wife defers to him, although their relationship is cold, stiff, and formal. But his children pay him little respect and are quick to explain why: "My dad's too uptight," says seventeen-year-old Bryan. "I wish he would lighten up, just once in his life." Brenda, fourteen, seconds the motion: "Daddy thinks too much. I remember one time I won a big race at our school's swim meet. I came home and told Daddy all about it. When I was finished he just sort of looked at me for a minute, and then said, 'I wonder when they're going to get around to building that new pool for you kids.' It was like he was on another planet!"

Emotionally, Allen might as well be! He is about as detached and emotionally unavailable as a father can get. Even when he says the right words ("I love you"; "Good job!"; "I'm sure proud of you"), the *feelings* are absent. Indeed, he withdraws from emotionally charged situations.

Some people view Allen as the ideal father. He provides for his family. He does his chores at home. He keeps his kids in line. He attends church faithfully. Yet there is no passion in the way he carries out these obligations. He seems to just go through the motions.

Allen distances himself from spontaneity to keep himself under control and not do anything "rash." For him, every decision must be well-considered; every action must be done "decently and in order." Unfortunately, Allen doesn't realize that this is just a cover, a rationalization for his own fear of emotion. In fact, he is probably not even capable of knowing what he feels at any given moment.

Allen is the product of a dysfunctional home in which emotions were not allowed. Unfortunately, he will remain distanced from his family *until* he seeks help to reawaken his capacity to listen to, own, and express his feelings.

THREE: DICTATORIAL HEADSHIP

John has an extremely high need to control. In fact, his idea of being "head of the household" means that nothing happens without his approval. Whenever his wife dares to question his authority or decisions, he resorts to intimidation tactics and then goes into a blind rage.

Not surprisingly, John treats his wife and kids like virtual slaves. He orders them around: "Take these shirts to the dry cleaners!" "Hey, where's my snack?!" "Son, get out there and mow the yard!" "This hamburger's fried to a crisp! Make me another!"

He also treats his wife according to sexual stereotypes. "It's a man's world," he loves to say, and acts as though it were. He likes the money his wife brings in from her job, yet criticizes her for being away rather than "at home where a woman belongs." If she does something that crosses him, he barks, "What a stupid thing to do! I guess that's all you can expect from a woman!" If his son breaks down in tears, he goes into a tirade. "Stop that crying," he orders, "and behave like a man!"

Never far away from physical violence, John gets his way by making threats. Anger is his chief emotion, and he bullies his family, unable to tolerate any opinion other than his own. Under certain circumstances he loses control and resorts to abuse. It is this fear that keeps his wife and kids in check, careful not to "rock the boat."

What's sad is that John sincerely believes he is leading his family according to biblical principles. While he has never examined the Bible's teaching in detail, he has a general conviction that God put men in charge. He picks and chooses what he wants to hear from Scripture.

The amazing thing is that John appears to be a "nice guy" to the outside world. At church he serves as an usher and once worked with the boy's club. At work he is often given demanding assignments; his boss knows he can be counted on to "get the job done." This popularity makes it especially hard for John to recognize how terribly unhealthy he is. He thinks that society approves of his behavior. The truth is, no one on the outside knows the real story.

TWO: WORKAHOLIC HEADSHIP

No one doubts David's ability to pay his way through life. As a young entrepreneur, he outworked everyone in the firm. Sometimes he started his day at four in the morning. He grew famous for such exploits. His associates admired his ability to get by on four or five hours of sleep. His competitors feared him as a relentless businessman who, if he couldn't outsmart them, would certainly outwork them.

David prides himself on being a self-made man. Ten years ago, his company rewarded his passion by making him president at age thirty-one — a remarkable achievement. The community admires him, too, for his savvy and success. And they have honored him by appointing him to a number of civic boards.

Unfortunately, there is a dark side to these business accolades. Work is more than a job to David. It's an obsession, an addiction. The people who feel the dark side most are his wife and two children.

At home, David's creative mind and visionary enterprise go dead. To him, home is a place to crash and burn for a while before the next meeting or business trip. It certainly is not a place of involvement. He just doesn't have the time or energy. In truth, he feels uncomfortable relating to his children or pursuing a deeper relationship with his wife. So he manages his household from a distance, parking them in a fashionable suburb with plenty of first-class amenities. He works like the dickens to pay for it all, priding himself on being an outstanding provider.

Though David is a regular churchgoer, Christian principles

have had little real impact on his view of his leadership role at home. Oh, occasionally he is pricked by a message on marriage or parenting. Then, he resolves to spend more "quality time" with his wife and kids. He may be prompted to attend a few of his kids' ball games or to take his wife on an exotic vacation. But these prove to be momentary guilt relievers rather than indications of a real change in his relationship to his family. Soon, David is back to his string of eighty-hour weeks.

Now that David's forty-one, his family is openly manifesting the effects of his workaholism. Cracks are appearing in what looked to outsiders to be a model home. When his wife complains that they are growing apart, David becomes defensive. He lists the things his work has done for her. He criticizes her for not being more supportive rather than blaming him for what he hasn't done. "Give me a break!" he shouts. His wife weeps over the creeping death of their relationship, but she can't get through to him. Nothing does.

Just last month, a close friend confronted David about spending more time with his two sons. Now that the boys are teenagers, the trouble spots in their lives are too obvious to ignore. David recently came down hard and grounded his fifteen-year-old for a month because of poor grades and drinking. Little does he know that his kids are simply mirroring his values and self-centered approach to life on an adolescent level.

David has no idea of the forces driving his life: greed, selfishness, insecurity, and so on. He has never taken the time to evaluate or reflect on the meaning of his life or ask significant questions about his motives. All this is expendable in the rush of work. For many men like David, it will take the pain of losing a wife or the foolishness and rebellion of children, or both, to reveal the ineptness of their leadership style. For now, the cheers of the community and the company have drowned out the cries for changes at home.

ONE: SPIRITUALLY APATHETIC HEADSHIP

To some women, Peter would make a fine husband. In fact, compared to the four men mentioned above, he seems to be an excellent catch. He works a steady job. He helps out around the house. He coaches his son's soccer team. And he goes to church pretty regularly.

So where's the problem? How is it that such a nice guy ends up as the number-one worst style of male leadership? What is it about Peter that drives his wife crazy?

The problem is not physical, emotional, financial, or sexual. It's spiritual. Peter is a believer and a church attender. But beyond that he's unresponsive to spiritual things. He never exercises spiritual leadership in his home. And that void blocks an intimacy his wife yearns for.

You see, Peter's wife, Marie, is a warm, caring woman who enjoys a vital, growing relationship with the Lord. She doesn't parade her faith in front of others, but quietly works behind the scenes in acts of mercy, kindness, and generosity. She loves the spiritual life she has found in Christ, but therein lies her pain.

As she listens to sermons Sunday after Sunday, Marie prays for her husband sitting beside her. She so badly wants him to respond in some way, to show any sign that God is at work in his life. On the way home she often asks him for a reaction to the message. Invariably he nods and says, "It was fine," then changes the subject.

That's the pattern for all of Peter's spiritual life. He never initiates prayer or by recalling a Scripture. He never reflects on life in terms of its spiritual dimension. As soon as talk turns to God or the Bible, he just tunes out. Sometimes he turns his attention away, sometimes he physically leaves.

Marie is heartbroken by Peter's apathy and lack of spiritual passion. And she feels frustrated and helpless to change him. Added to that is the deep loneliness she feels in not being able to share this special part of her life with the person she loves the most.

Today, too many women feel like Marie. It's epidemic. As a pastor, I can tell you that I've met countless women like her and heard about their disappointment in this area. That's why I place the spiritually apathetic husband as the number-one "head"-ache.

Is There Hope for the Headless Marriage?
Keep in mind that these are just my "Top Five" profiles of "leaderlessness." I could mention other ways that men fall down in their responsibilities, leaving their families "headless." But these five represent some of the major abuses that occur when men misapply

or just plain ignore the Bible's teaching on male leadership in the home. It's not that these men are evil. But they are inflicting great evils on their wives and children by these unbiblical behaviors.

If you as a husband recognize yourself in one or more of these examples, what can you do to change? Is there hope for you and your marriage? Yes, there is! In the next chapter I'll suggest several things you can do to restore Christlike leadership to your family.

20

Is There Hope
for the Headless Family?

In the last chapter, I painted five graphic pictures of what unbiblical male leadership looks like. I did that because most men tend to respond to things that are concrete. "Headship" is an abstraction; but hugging our wives, paying the bills, showing up for work, and buying a new van are all concrete things most of us can understand.

I hope that as you've looked at these matters you've been challenged to ask yourself: How am I doing as a leader in my home? Am I a lording leader or a serving leader? Do I exhibit any of the five negative leadership styles? Are there changes I need to make in the way I treat my wife and kids?

If you've been asking yourself any similar questions, let me offer some suggestions for how you can get started. In a way you have already begun by asking how you can be a better husband. You've taken a major step forward, perhaps the hardest step for a man to take.

You see, most of us as men prefer to make excuses, blame others, and evade responsibility. Our problems are always "out there"! We hate to admit that *we* must change, that the problem is in us! But when we finally face ourselves squarely and accept responsibility for what we've become, then we're ready to take steps toward growth.

Two Steps You Can Take

How can you start to be a better servant-leader? Let me offer two simple suggestions. First, *increase your knowledge base.* We saw in 1 Peter 3:7 the challenge to live with our wives "in an understanding way," literally, "according to knowledge." How much do you know about women in general? I'm not talking about the kind of "knowledge" that guys pick up in high school locker rooms or around water coolers at work. How much objective, healthy information about women have you considered? You'll treat your wife altogether differently as you come to understand the cloth from which she's cut.

There are a number of excellent resources available to help you. Several times I've mentioned the well-written, practical book by Dr. James Dobson, *What Wives Wish Their Husbands Knew About Women.* That's a start. I know that some of you may not like to read. But if you're serious about upgrading your leadership skills, you'll make the effort as a way to understand your wife.

A second thing you can do is *join or form a small group* of other men for interaction, prayer, and accountability. We men are such Lone Rangers. We love to go it alone. But what we need to realize is how much we need each other's support, wisdom, accountability, and experience. I would even go so far as to say that having the challenge of facing other men is *essential* in order to live up to the commitments we've made in marriage.

Look around at your church or where you work for two or three other Christian men who want to grow as leaders in their homes. Get together weekly to share your stories and your struggles. Pray for each other, and support each other as you seek to make changes. Perhaps you could use this book or one of the others I've suggested as a way to start discussing these issues.

Professional Help

Books and support groups are excellent ways for any man to get started in the process of changing his leadership style. But some of us face needs and problems that go *far beyond* the scope of these resources. We struggle with serious, long-term troubles that do more than just hamper our marriages—they threaten to undo our relationships entirely. What sort of help should a man in that type of situation seek?

I wish there were an easy answer. But men today struggle with such a wide array of problems, and there are so many different kinds of services available, that no one, simple answer will serve. However, whatever help you obtain should fit three important criteria.

First, it should be *professional.* As you consider the services of a counselor, psychologist, or other professional, you need to ask: What sort of expertise does this person have? What are his training and credentials? What experience and track record can he demonstrate? Just because someone calls himself a "counselor" is no guarantee of competence, particularly in the Christian community. Your personal health and the health of your marriage are too important to be left to amateurs. Seek out someone qualified to help you work through your problems.

In addition, look for help that is *biblical.* That doesn't mean that the person has to have a seminary or Bible college education. But it is important that his methods and advice be consistent with the overall teaching of Scripture. While the field of psychology has provided valuable insights and techniques related to human behavior, we need to honor God's Word as our ultimate authority.

Finally, look for help that is *long-term.* This is perhaps the hardest criterion for most men to accept. We desire immediate results and the quick fix. But health doesn't come that way. Dysfunctional behavior is learned over a lifetime, so it will likely take many years to unlearn it. Change happens one day at a time, over time. Anyone who promises to "heal" you or "deliver" you from your problems in one or two simple sessions is highly suspect.

Sure, we've all heard stories of the alcoholic or drug addict miraculously "healed" in an instant of prayer. But that is crisis intervention, not long-term healing. The person still has a *lot* of deeper, chronic issues to take care of, things that probably got him into trouble in the first place. Lasting change happens over the long haul.

WHAT CAN YOU DO AS A WIFE?

What if you are the wife of a man like those described in the previous chapter? Is there anything you can do to promote change in your husband? The answer is an unqualified *no!* You cannot change your husband. Nor is that your responsibility. Only he can make changes in himself. But that doesn't mean you have to put up with his unhealth. You do not have to be a victim. Your role has nothing to do with accepting abuse or the irresponsibility in your husband.

For example, if your husband physically abuses you, you need to seek help right away. If he hits you, slaps you, shakes you, twists your arm, slams you against the wall, forces himself sexually on you, or in any other way causes physical or emotional pain, you need help. If you go through cycles in which your husband tenses up over little things, then eventually lashes out at you with physical violence, and finally dismisses the episode by blaming you or giving excuses ("I had a little too much to drink"; "I was just tired"; "I didn't really hit you that hard"), you need help. If he physically, sexually, or emotionally mistreats the children, you need help.

Your community may have a hotline for battered women. If so, call it. They will offer advice, support, and refuge. Your pastor or the pastor of another church may also be able to suggest resources. Your doctor will know of some.

In addition, there are numerous books that provide insight and understanding into this problem. I recommend these two: Kay Marshall Strom's *In the Name of Submission: A Painful Look at Wife Battering;* and *Battered into Submission* by James and Phyllis Alsdurf. These are available through a Christian bookstore.

The worst thing you can do is to deny that your husband is abusing you or keep quiet about it. Don't be tricked into believing that you somehow "deserve" the punishment he gives you. You don't! Nor should you shy away from taking action, perhaps because of your husband's position in the community, or because you assume that "nothing can be done." Your husband may never change, but you *can* make changes to protect yourself and your children. However, if you do nothing, you are actually encouraging the abuse.

SERIOUS BUSINESS

Before moving on, I want to remind all of us that leadership in the home is serious business. I've presented my "Top Five" list of "leaderless" profiles, but the reality behind these behaviors is no laughing matter. Unless a man commits himself to Christ's model of headship, and unless he pursues spiritual and emotional health, in time he's likely to fall into one of the dysfunctional patterns I've already mentioned. When that happens, his wife and children usually fall with him.

21

"Helper" Doesn't Mean "Enabler"

A breakdown of male leadership in the home is usually replaced by some ugly substitutes: physical and emotional abuse, manipulation, evasion of responsibility, and similar kinds of unhealth.

However, tragedies like that don't just happen. In nearly every instance that I'm aware of where a husband's behavior has severely damaged the marriage, the wife has had a hand in creating or at least perpetuating the problem. Counselors refer to this behavior as "enabling." The wife acts in a way that actually promotes her husband's unhealth. She may be completely unaware of how she contributes to the problem. She may even think she is helping the situation. But actually her efforts only assist her husband to continue in his dysfunctional pattern.

CAROL AND JACK

Let me illustrate. Carol's husband, Jack, was accused of having an affair with a coworker. The woman's husband confronted Jack and his boss with several pieces of reliable evidence implicating him in the liaison. More importantly, the woman herself admitted to being intimate with Jack on several occasions.

Yet Jack denies any sexual involvement. He says that he "made a mistake" in becoming emotionally attached to the woman, and "probably went too far" in expressing his affection. But he emphatically insists that nothing sexual ever occurred. Carol chooses to believe Jack rather than the information that has trickled back to her. "If Jack says nothing happened, then nothing happened," she snaps. "Why does everyone have to believe the woman's story? Why can't they trust Jack?"

Carol never asks for a complete review of the evidence by a third party. She never presses Jack on the details about his side of the story. She never seeks out the opinion of a counselor. In fact, she closes ranks with Jack and becomes his most loyal supporter. She justifies her actions in the name of love and support. "I'm learning that it's in the tough times like this that a man really needs his wife the most," she says. "Our relationship has never been stronger."

What makes Carol's behavior so suspect is that this is not the first time she has faced this sort of problem. Shortly after she and Jack were married, he was fired from his job when his boss learned that he had seduced a client. Jack claimed it was all "a big misunderstanding," and Carol never investigated. A few years later, Carol came home unexpectedly from her job one morning to find Jack and a female neighbor sitting together on the couch. Nothing sexual appeared to be going on, but the situation looked odd. Jack claimed that the woman "just had some questions she wanted to ask me." He never explained why he was home and not at his job.

Other incidents have taken place that would lead an objective person to ask: What's going on with this guy? Is he telling the truth? Is he being unfaithful to his wife? But Carol is not objective. She is dependent on her relationship with Jack—too dependent. She is afraid to know the truth. She denies a lot of obvious clues that something is wrong, not only in Jack, but in her marriage. Yet by closing her eyes to it all and defending him, she is *enabling* him to continue in his sin and unhealth.

Why would a wife do such a thing? Ultimately, it's because she herself has some unhealthy patterns. Carol, for instance, grew up in a family where conflict and confrontation were not allowed. Consequently, she is too weak to challenge Jack, even if she has doubts. Even worse, she doesn't allow herself to feel any doubt because the possibility that her husband might be unfaithful is simply too painful for her to accept. Besides, what would happen to her and her children if she confronted this? Security is an overriding concern for her. So is her dream to have an ideal marriage. She would rather pretend that adultery can't happen than face the reality that it likely has happened.

BUT DOESN'T THE BIBLE SAY . . . ?

I'm afraid there are many "enablers" like Carol. Enabling is a classic mistake always wrapped with the best of intentions. But it doesn't solve the problem. It intensifies it. Perhaps the greatest tragedy is that so many of these wives use the Bible to rationalize their enabling behavior. Just as some husbands use Scripture to justify behaviors that are abusive, selfish, immature, or immoral, some wives justify their enabling as biblical. They often reason they are "following God's will," even as they allow themselves and their families to be mistreated.

For instance, a woman will put up with a husband who physically abuses her in the mistaken belief that "submission" demands that she do so. In fact, some pastors and Bible teachers applaud her for enduring with a "gentle and quiet spirit." What an outrageous misuse of Scripture! Biblical submission has absolutely nothing to do with that sort of behavior. Biblical submission means helping a man act as the responsible leader God intends him to be. It never encourages a woman to promote and enable unhealth and sin.

STEPS YOU CAN TAKE

In Psalm 139, David asks God to help him make a fearless inventory of his life. He prays (verses 23-24),

> *Search me, O God. . . .*
> *Try me. . . .*
> *And see if there be any hurtful way in me,*
> *And lead me in the everlasting way.*

I want to urge every wife to be just as spiritually aggressive. Open your eyes to signs of unhealth in yourself, your husband, and your marriage, and have the courage to admit any problems that may be there. God is the Master at helping His children work out their troubles, but not if they pretend that problems don't exist. Profound, lasting change comes to those who face their problems and with God's help take action!

I also encourage you to team up with other women for prayer and encouragement. It's the isolated woman who is most at risk for enabling behavior. A group of other women can help you "define reality" by offering objectivity and perspective.

Some wives are up against forces that require more serious, and even professional, help. You should seek that kind of help if any of the following conditions apply to your marriage:

1. If there is physical abuse of any kind, either by you or your husband, toward any member of the family.
2. If you are afraid to speak your own mind or express your feelings.
3. If you take responsibility for your husband's behavior or his feelings (for example, if you blame yourself when he gets angry).
4. If you make excuses or "cover" for your husband's behavior (for example, if you call in sick for him when he is hung over).
5. If there is any sexual infidelity, aberration, or manipulation.
6. If you feel guilt or shame over the way your husband treats you.
7. If there are addictions or substance abuses of any kind (for example, alcohol, drugs, pornography, sex, gambling, even work).
8. If there is chronic debt, chronic unemployment, or frequent changes from job to job.
9. If there are constant, chronic arguments and conflict.
10. If weeks or months go by without serious, heart-to-heart talks between you and your husband concerning any serious problems you believe are present in your relationship.

LOOKING FOR HELP

Where can you turn for help? That depends on the nature and extent of the problem. But in most areas of our country, there are many resources available to you. A minister, priest, or doctor may be able to point you in the right direction. Many churches have special programs addressing some of the needs mentioned in the list above.

A marriage counselor may be helpful, if (and it's a big "if") you and your husband are *both* committed to working together on problems in your relationship. Likewise, a psychologist or psychiatrist may be useful in helping you deal with deep-seated, long-term problems that seem to defy resolution.

A related resource is a small therapy group run by a psychologist or social worker. A group can be invaluable in helping you clarify the way things *really* are, and the different personalities involved can enable you to understand yourself in a more complete way. Many specialized agencies have discovered how valuable the group experience can be. Support groups now exist for any number of specific disorders—for example, Alcoholics Anonymous, AlAnon, codependency groups, and other Twelve-Step programs.

In addition to these, there are shelters for battered wives and abused children; drug abuse hotlines and treatment centers; suicide prevention hotlines; programs offered by your employer or your husband's employer; and your doctor, lawyer, accountant, and similar professionals.

Perhaps this list of potential helpers seems obvious. But I offer it anyway, if only to give permission to women to seek help if they need it. As a pastor, I'm all too aware of a woman's tendency to deny that a problem exists, and also to suffer in silence when she is paralyzed by the thought of confrontation. Even worse, she may spiritualize the issue: "If only I pray harder, things will get better. If only I become more spiritual, my husband will change. If only I have more faith, it will all work out. If only. . . ."

Sometimes after a woman has left my office, I find myself saying "if only," too. If only this woman would *help* her husband and *stop* enabling him! Certainly a wife needs to pray, but she also needs to act. In seeking help, some women actually begin to be a real help to their husbands for the first time.

Finally, let me offer one additional piece of advice. Don't be afraid to get more than one opinion about the nature of your problem and the course of action you should take. In "an abundance of counselors there is victory" (Proverbs 11:14). This also provides much needed security and reassurance when contemplating tough steps of action!

WOMEN IN DISTRESS

In James 1:27, we read that "pure and undefiled religion" is "to visit orphans and widows in their distress." A woman who loses her husband is a woman in distress. Unfortunately, not only death or divorce causes the loss of a man. Whenever a husband fails to fulfill his role of servant-leadership, his wife and family will suffer. In a very real way, they have lost the man they need. In fact, the very person who is supposed to protect them has, through his irresponsibility, become the one who distresses them.

Husbands, if you are distressing your family, get help! Have the courage to accept responsibility for your behavior, and seek out someone to help you make changes. God will honor you for it.

Wives, be on your guard against enabling your husband to "get away" with irresponsible, abusive behaviors. God calls you to be his "helper," but helper doesn't mean enabler. So, don't be! Even if your man resists making changes, take responsibility for yourself and look for help. Do it now! God doesn't ask you to suffer in silence, especially when He has provided so many resources to help you in your distress.

One of the most important of those resources is the church. There's so much to say about that, however, I've devoted the next chapter to discussing it.

22

The Church:
Can It Be a Refuge for Women?

In her powerful book *In the Name of Submission,* Kay Marshall Strom told about an abused woman who sought the advice of her pastor:

> "After my husband beat me for the third time in a month, I turned in desperation to my minister," said Pamela. "I wish I hadn't. First, he assured me my husband was not a bad man and meant me no harm. Then he instructed me to be more tolerant, more understanding, and to forgive my husband for beating me, just as Christ forgave those who beat him. I went home determined to do better, but I was greeted at the door by a punch in the face. How much must I tolerate? Does Christ really want me to stay in an abusive relationship?"[1]

The answer is an unqualified *No!* My heart breaks for Pamela and the thousands of women like her who have been told to go home and submit to sick, abusive men. If this is an accurate report of what her minister said, he mishandled the Scripture and contributed to nothing less than wife abuse!

I wish this were an isolated case, but it isn't. Far too often churches look the other way when husbands act unbiblically. The pastors and leaders know something is wrong, but except for the most extreme cases of sexual misconduct or physical abuse, they do nothing. You see, churches can be enablers, too! What a contrast to the interdependent community of believers exhorted in the New Testament to aggressively address unhealthy marriages - (1 Corinthians 5) and sinful behaviors (Matthew 18). This certainly included steps to help a woman whose husband chronically failed his wife and family.[2]

We need to return to that era of "tough love." Surely God will judge those of us who are church leaders if we fail to "shepherd the flock of God . . . according to the will of God" (1 Peter 5:2). Without question, one reason God gives a woman a husband is for protection. But if the protector himself turns out to be an irresponsible or worthless fellow, then other believers need to step in and offer her protection and other help (Galatians 6:1-2).

A CLIMATE FOR GROWING HEALTHY FAMILIES

What can the church do? First, a church needs to cultivate an overall community of believers that encourages healthy marriages. In the New Testament, Paul told Pastor Titus to "speak the things which are fitting for sound doctrine" (Titus 2:1), "speak and exhort and reprove with all authority. Let no one disregard you" (2:15). The context shows that a major theme of Titus' ministry was to be marital relations.[3]

In the same way, pastors ought to teach on biblical roles from the pulpit. Their teaching should be clear and uncompromising. It also should be "wholistic"—that is, reflecting the whole counsel of God, not just a few favorite texts. In my opinion, today's church could stand a lot more preaching to husbands about their role as servant-leaders. Women would benefit from hearing the wife's role as helper expanded and clarified.

In addition to its pulpit ministry, the church should sponsor classes and seminars offering couples practical strategies for building their families according to biblical principles. There is no end to books, workbooks, discussion guides, video series, and other materials devoted to marriage and family issues. Husbands especially need to be recruited to participate in small groups that discuss marriage and family issues. Men need to become account-able to one another for follow through.

ACCOUNTABILITY

The things I mentioned above are all positive ways to encourage men to become the leaders God expects them to be. But there is second strategy that is more challenging: Churches need to treat men according to biblical expectations for conduct and character. In 1 Timothy 3, Paul spells out very specific standards by which Christian men should be evaluated.[4] Some people will say that these are standards for leaders, and of course they are. But the New Testament knows no double standard, one for leaders and one for "lay people." Rather, there is one standard. Those in leadership should be living it, and everyone else should be striving for it.

One key area evaluated in 1 Timothy 3 is a man's relationship to his wife and family (verses 4-5,12):

> He must be one who manages his own household well, keep-ing his children under control with all dignity (but if a man does not know how to manage his own household, how will he take care of the church of God?). . . . Let deacons be hus-bands of only one wife, and good managers of their children and their own households.

The church has a responsibility to pay close attention to this and challenge men to Christlikeness. Practically speaking, that means many churches today need to stop enabling men to mistreat their wives by letting them continue in unhealthy behavior. For starters, churches need to prevent men from teaching and from serving on boards and committees who are known to be selfish, abusive, chronically absent, and irresponsible. Remember, as lead-ers go, so go the people.

Let's not forget, too, that the pastor himself should be held to these same accountabilities. I'm afraid there are times when churches and Christian organizations enable their leaders to get away with behavior that they would quickly condemn in anyone else. In some cases, entire institutions are built around and reinforce one man's unhealth. There is but one standard for Christian character and conduct, and Scripture, specifically 1 Timothy 3, spells it out. Those who intend to be leaders should be above reproach in living up to that standard.

Unfortunately, some pastors pull back from confronting a man who happens to be a large donor to the church, or one who holds a position of power. That is nothing but cowardice, unworthy of a servant of Christ. It's also unethical because it is nothing less than winking at sin for financial gain.

The same is true for the pastor who goes easy on his buddies in the church. For instance, he may know that one of his close friends is neglecting his family because of overcommitment at the office. The pastor may even mention his concern to this man. But when the fellow explains it away or changes the subject, the pastor doesn't press the issue. He steps back for fear of what further confrontation may mean.

This is pastoral enablement! It excuses leaven that in time will leaven the whole lump (Galatians 5:9). This is a far cry from Paul's calling to his young pastor friend Titus (2:15):

> Speak and exhort and reprove with all authority. Let no one disregard you.

No one! Not friends, not the rich, not anybody! Likewise, he tells Timothy (1 Timothy 5:21):

> I solemnly charge you in the presence of God and of Christ Jesus and of His chosen angels, to maintain these principles without bias, doing nothing in a spirit of partiality.

Paul sounds pretty serious. That's because accountability is serious stuff! And it applies to *everyone* in the Church. Confrontation takes courage. But pastoral courage is a much-needed commodity today.

TAKING ACTION

There is a third step that the church can take in coming to the aid of wives, and that is *direct action* on their behalf. There are a couple of levels at which this can happen: crisis intervention and long-term programs of help. Not every church will be able to offer long-term resources (for example, professional counseling, support groups, and so on), but it certainly should be prepared for intervention. The common term for this action is "church discipline," but I personally think a more accurate description is "church restoration."

This step-by-step process, as outlined in Scripture, can be used to call a wayward husband back to a responsible lifestyle.[5] I'm going to devote the entire next chapter to a "case study" along these lines. In many instances, church restoration can be a powerful force for rescuing a failing marriage. Of course, it is not an easy process. But our churches and marriages would be healthier if we paid more attention to Scripture on this issue.

It's important to realize that crisis intervention is only a first step in bringing change to troubled marriages. It guarantees nothing. Lasting results usually come from long-term programs, consistently helping people over an extended period of time.

I'm encouraged to see more churches setting up the kinds of support groups and other resources I mentioned in the last chapter. I would never want to see the Church depart from her primary purpose of declaring the gospel and helping believers grow through worship, instruction, and community. But churches must provide structures where the truth they proclaim can be tried, practiced, and implemented. Biblically focused programs similar to Twelve-Step and growth groups, along with personal discipling, can help that happen.

LIZ AND ROGER

Even though this chapter is seeking to encourage the Church's support and help for hurting wives, let me offer one caution: Watch out for the woman who wants the church to side with her, rather than helping her take responsibility for herself. There's a big difference! Unfortunately, this is one of the most common problems churches face in attempting to help women.

Liz is a good example. She began attending our church, sometimes bringing her husband, Roger, but usually coming alone. She joined a women's Bible study and really seemed to be growing spiritually.

One day, Liz phoned the church office and asked to see one of the pastors right away. I arranged to meet with her that afternoon.

As soon as our appointment began, she blurted out, "I can't take it anymore. I'm seriously considering leaving Roger."

I could tell she was in tremendous pain, so I asked her to tell me more. She gave me a lengthy history of her relationship with Roger. She said that Roger was manipulative, always getting what he wanted. He worked too much. He never complimented her or told her that he loved her. Their sex life was dead. She thought that he might have a mistress. Most of all, he showed no interest in spiritual things. She doubted that he was even a believer. We talked for several hours about their situation.

I'm not sure Liz really wanted help for her marriage. What became clear was that she felt she had done all she could. In a nondirective way, she was actually seeking my approval. I felt very uncomfortable for her and for me. Many pastors find themselves in this hard seat. On the one hand, Liz was probably giving me a fairly accurate picture of Roger. Her pain was real. But on the other hand, I sensed that she had not been very responsible, either. Her description of how she had responded to Roger over the years seemed to confirm that. Liz needed help, too!

"Why don't you arrange for both of you to meet with me, and we can talk about it together with Roger?" I suggested. "You don't need to leave him. What you need is help—real help."

Liz looked uncomfortable, as though I had trapped her. She seemed reluctant to accept my willingness to get involved, but then agreed.

An appointment was set for the next week, and I thought carefully about what I needed to do and say. But one thing I didn't count on was Liz not showing up! When the time came, Roger was there, but there was no sign of Liz. Finally, I decided to begin without her. "Roger, let me tell you why Liz wanted this meeting," I said. "She's thinking about leaving you."

Roger, a powerfully built, trim, well-dressed man, was crushed. He seemed to be baffled as to why his wife would do this. Sure, he realized there were problems in their marriage. He confessed that much of what Liz had said about him was true. It also was not hard to discern that Roger was extremely manipulative. But he never thought Liz would leave him. He assured me he was willing to get help. He would do whatever he could to save his marriage, even long-term counseling. He was willing to start immediately.

That day I called Liz at her workplace. I told her how disappointed I felt because she hadn't kept the appointment. I also told her Roger had not been fully aware of how serious their problems were or how deeply hurt she was. He had agreed to enter counseling.

That didn't sit well with her. "I can't believe you let him manipulate you like that!" she cried. "Now he has you on his side!"

I explained that I had no interest in taking sides. But it was no use — she had stopped listening. Finally she just hung up.

The next Sunday Roger came to church. He told me that Liz had packed her things and left. He felt certain she was gone for good.

Without Liz, Roger saw no use for the counseling. He still attends our church but shows few signs of growth. I've noticed that he uses his divorce from Liz to gain support and sympathy from other people. He is still manipulating. In a way, I feel helpless. Liz has never been back to our church, and I doubt we'll ever see her again. I grieve for her.

There is much to be learned from this story. But I want to emphasize that the church can do little for a person — man or woman — who doesn't want to be helped.

Liz had let her troubled marriage simmer for years before it finally boiled over and she left. During all that time, she didn't use the many resources that were available to her. Instead, she just suffered in silence. Over time, she became mistrustful of other people. That's why, when I proposed long-term counseling, she resisted and accused me of taking sides, instead of making an effort at change. She didn't want to go through the process. She no longer had the energy.

Today, she's still enabling Roger, even from a distance. By walking away from the marriage, she gave him exactly what he wanted — the sympathy and support of other people. Liz set herself up to be a victim.

Meanwhile, people in my church are confused. Some of the women know Liz. They're aware of the troubles she had in the relationship. But they're disappointed that she's cut herself off. Her behavior raises questions about her credibility. Meanwhile, Roger hangs around and enjoys the attention he gets, playing the situation to his advantage as "the poor, abandoned husband."

There's not much a church can do in a situation like that. No one can force a woman to get help who has set herself up to be a victim. Not me, not the church, not even God. No one can live our lives for us.

23
Church Intervention: A Case Study

In the last chapter we saw that a church has an important, biblically defined role to play in coming to the assistance of a woman whose husband chronically and willfully falls down in his leadership responsibilities. Now I want to describe one case that illustrates this process.

A woman in our church—let me call her Cheri—came to see one of our pastors about her husband, Paul.[1] Paul had great difficulty holding down a steady job. It was a situation that had gone on for years. He also chronically mismanaged the couple's finances, with the result that he and Cheri had to file for bankruptcy. But, even after that, he continued to act recklessly and irresponsibly.

When the pastor met with Cheri and Paul together, Paul admitted his wife's report was true. A number of practical suggestions were made and agreed on, and some long-term assistance was set up with the enlistment of a counselor. However, within a matter of months Paul was back to his old ways. He skipped the counseling appointments and continued to abuse the finances. Before long he was out of work again.

When Cheri reported this to the pastor, he and one of our elders set up a meeting with Paul to review the situation. Once again, specific conditions were set forth, and Paul agreed to make changes. But again it was all talk. The situation only grew worse. More than six months passed.

At this point, we as church leaders realized Paul and Cheri needed more than just counseling—she needed men to back her up if she chose to stand up to Paul's irresponsibility. Paul needed a special kind of help if he was ever to have a chance at real change.

After a great deal of prayer and discussion, Cheri arranged a meeting between herself, Paul, one of our pastors, and two of our elders. With the help of a counselor in our church, she drafted the following letter, which she read to Paul at the meeting:

> First I want to tell you that *I love you very much.* Our marriage is very important to me and I want it to be happy, healthy, whole, and long. There are some things you are doing that are destroying my love for you, and I want to address those things while there is still love in my heart for you and to give you the opportunity to choose how to respond to that love while you still have a choice.
>
> The problem is your lack of assuming financial responsibility for our family. I have listed eight evidences of that here. These are a few of the types of things that are totally unacceptable to me. This is not a complete list, but rather a sampling.
>
> 1. You spent $560 last year on a rifle and hunting equipment, leaving medical bills unpaid.
> 2. You left a salaried position to go into business for yourself with no savings for our family to live on.
> 3. You neglected to file quarterly taxes in that business as required by law, resulting in a tax debt of several hundred dollars.
> 4. You were jobless for five of the last twenty-four months.
> 5. You used a company car for a personal vacation—knowingly violating company policy—resulting in the loss of your job.
> 6. You have borrowed a total of $2,800 from your father

without establishing a repayment plan.

7. You have become three months delinquent in our daughter's tuition and have failed to contact the school, placing the burden of accountability on my shoulders.

8. You have refused to participate faithfully in financial counseling made available to us at no charge.

As a result of the financial and emotional destruction that has taken place and as a means of preventing further damage, I have established with the help of the pastors three very basic requirements that you must agree to this morning, and they are as follows:

1. You must bring home each month at least the amount that I contribute to our household, which is $1,750. If during the next thirty days you are unable to do that at your present job, you will have thirty days to find one or more hourly wage or salaried positions that will enable you to do that.

2. You must commit to TOTAL financial honesty and accountability through two resources for a *minimum* of two years. First, through Christian Money Management, to establish a budget and plan to address our debt. Second, through a Christian businessman in our church who will oversee and work through any job, venture, or business decisions you have to make.

3. You must agree to immediately begin both long-term personal and marriage counseling.

To be fair, I need to tell you what I will do if you choose at any time not to follow through with these requirements.

1. Your failure to provide for our family in the way specified will be your decision to live separately from our family.

2. In the future, a thirty-day time lapse in providing for our family in the way specified or refusal to follow through with any part of the above requirements will be understood as your decision to live separately from our family.

3. In the event you choose through your actions or inactions to live elsewhere, a petition for separate maintenance will be filed and the locks on our house will be changed.

All of these action points have the approval and backing of our church leadership. Now I need to know if these requirements are acceptable to you.

If they are not, we will have an appointment with the attorney on Monday and the locks will be changed today on our home.

It took a great deal of courage for Cheri to draft that letter, challenging her husband to assume his biblical responsibilities. After years of carrying the family financially and covering for Paul's problem, she finally was fulfilling her role as a helper by offering this "tough love."

I was proud of our church for standing with Cheri in this difficult situation. We had linked her with numerous resources—a marriage counselor, a Christian financial counselor, an elder with business savvy and common sense, legal counsel—and we were prepared to mobilize additional resources if necessary, including financial help. Of course we were also praying regularly for her and Paul.

This is just one example of how a church can draw alongside a woman in distress. It allowed Cheri to make some real, vital changes for the first time. In doing so, I submit that she was also offering real help to her husband. In a number of cases like Cheri's, this type of intervention has worked. At the time of this writing, she and Paul are separated, but for the first time in their marriage they are beginning to move toward one another with real change. The twenty-plus years of playing games are over, and hope has been rekindled.

FOR DISCUSSION

1. Define the terms "helper" and "enabler" in your own words. What's the difference between these two words? Wives, be honest: Are you an enabler in your marriage relationship? How can

you take that quality and make it healthy — becoming a helper to your husband and children?

Husbands, do you count on your wife to enable you? Have you asked her to support behavior that's inappropriate or unethical in the name of "submission"?

2. Read 1 Corinthians 5:1-13 and Matthew 18:15-20. Discuss what you think couples should do when the wife is an enabler, or the husband allows (or forces) his wife to enable inappropriate, unbiblical behavior. How should churches be responding when they become aware of inappropriate behavior in a marriage relationship (such as abuse, adultery, or even absenteeism)?

3. Read 1 Timothy 3:4-5,12. What concrete responsibilities do you see here that husbands are supposed to fulfill? Do you recognize any ways to escape those responsibilities? How do wives hinder husbands from following the duties outlined in these verses? Can the wife actually enable her husband to avoid these responsibilities? How can wives support their husbands to fulfill the duties listed here?

4. Read the list of conditions under the heading "Steps You Can Take" in chapter 21. Do you have any serious problems like this in your marriage relationship? If so, who could you turn to?

5. The word "accountability" gets thrown about easily these days. What is the local church's role in holding husbands and wives accountable in their marriages? What role can couples in healthy marriages take to foster accountability and help others build stronger marriages?

6. Chapter 19 listed the top five "Headaches": irresponsible headship, emotionally detached headship, dictatorial headship, workaholic headship, and spiritually apathetic headship. Husbands, do you recognize any of these problems in the way you lead your family? Wives, do you see any of these problems in your husband's leadership? What can you do about them? Do you know an older couple whose marriage seems healthy and who might be able to mentor you? Or, can you talk to your pastor — at least for a referral for more professional help in these areas? If you're concerned about your own pastor's response, is there another pastor in your community who you can talk to for counseling or for a referral?

Part Eight

PRACTICAL APPLICATIONS

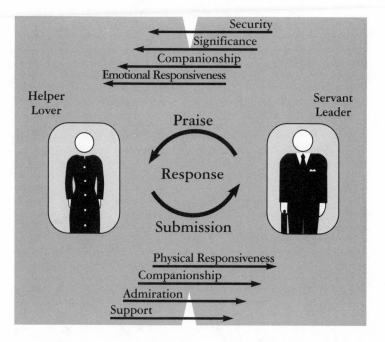

24

Forget-Me-Nots

If you ever want to spark a lively discussion at a dinner party, just mention the subject of this book—roles in marriage. There's enough controversy and emotion to get everyone involved! But if you want to generate some real heat, introduce the issue of working wives, especially working mothers with young children. That's a guaranteed explosion!

The fact is, women themselves are deeply divided on this issue. On the one hand, many employed mothers feel tremendous guilt about leaving their kids while they work. On the other hand, many women who stay at home feel slighted by society. As a result, "You can't talk to all women in the same way," says Judsen Culbreath, editor-in-chief of *Working Mother* magazine. "By targeting one group, you can alienate the other."[1]

I'm not interested in alienating anyone with this book. If you're a woman, I want to help you discover the vital role God has given you to play in your family and in society. The Bible never prohibits you from working outside the home. Indeed, first-century women apparently were employed as extensively as women are today; and the New Testament never told them to quit their jobs. Still, it appears that they also struggled with tensions between work and family.

Does Scripture address that tension? Not directly. In fact, it says very little about a woman's work outside the home.[2] But it does emphasize the priorities, values, and roles that she should use in making lifestyle decisions. This is important to realize because the work issue is complex. There's no one right answer to fit every situation. Each woman and each family needs to determine what is best for them, using biblical guidelines.

What are those guidelines? In this and the next two chapters, let me suggest three principles you as a woman can use in considering work-related issues.

God expects you as a wife to fulfill your core role, whether or not you work outside the home.

Titus 2:4-5, among other passages, describes a wife's core role as "husband-lover" and "child-lover." Keep in mind that *core role* refers to the essential function God has designed you to fulfill in your marriage. That role is not all that you do in marriage. But it provides structure and direction. You can't ignore your fundamental role without creating heartache for yourself, your husband, and your family.

"Husband-lover"—we looked at that assignment in some detail in chapter 12. As Genesis 2 makes clear, God has created you to be a "helper" to your spouse, someone who completes him and supplies what he lacks.

Does that responsibility change if you decide to work outside the home? There's no indication in Scripture that it does. On the contrary, Proverbs 31—a description of the "ideal" Hebrew wife—actually reinforces the husband-loving role. Though she handles many activities outside the home, the Proverbs 31 wife remains focused on her husband and her home. He can trust her, the passage says, because "she does him good and not evil all the days of her life" (verse 12). In short, "She looks well to the ways of her household" (verse 27).

The challenge for Christian wives today is to pay attention to the needs of their husbands. We rightly condemn a man who works too much, neglecting his wife and children. Scripture never approves of that. By the same token, a woman who neglects her husband or children in order to work outside the home is violating a basic biblical principle. The issue is not whether she should be employed, but whether she is fulfilling her responsibilities at home.

By the way, a woman doesn't have to go outside the home to ignore the needs of her husband. A nonemployed mother can devote so much energy and attention to her children that she overlooks her husband. When it comes to her time, affection, interest, and other helping capacities, he gets the leftovers. This is just as much a failure of core responsibility as when a wife works in a paid position to the detriment of her family.

WORK AND CHILDREN

A wife's core responsibilities do not end with her husband. She also is called to be a "child-lover." Here we come to the emotional heart of the issue of working women. What about the children of the woman in the workforce, especially when they are of preschool age?

I'm afraid our society is not giving women much help in answering that question. Perhaps it just doesn't want to face the reality that kids need mommies, despite overwhelming evidence that they do. According to one expert:

> It has been determined that children who do not have the benefit of a single, sustained contact with a loving mother-figure for at least the first three years of their lives will, depending on the degree of deprivation, manifest a diminished capacity to love others, impaired intellectual powers, and an inability to control their impulses, especially in the area of aggression.[3]

Healthy, normal child development demands a primary caregiver. Can daycare provide that? In the late seventies, psychologists indicated that it could, and promoted daycare as the alternative of choice for working mothers. In fact, some suggested that daycare could actually benefit children from poorer homes. One prominent researcher who held such a view was Penn State's Jay Belsky.

Belsky has now reversed himself. After years of follow-up studies, he has concluded that babies who spend more than twenty hours a week in non-maternal care during the first year of life risk developing an "insecure attachment" to their mothers. He says the evidence shows that such children are more likely to be uncooperative and aggressive in early school years.

Psychiatrist Peter Barglow of Chicago's Michael Reese Hospital concurs. His studies indicate that upper-middle-class one-year-olds who are cared for by expensive nannies and babysitters tend to be less securely attached to their mothers.[4]

Clearly, babies appear to do best when tended by one person, ideally a parent. "Is the mother by far the best caretaker for the child in the first year? We think probably yes," says Barglow.[5]

Yet you'd never know that by looking at today's work force. More than 60 percent of U.S. households have two incomes—that means working moms.[6]

What do most of these parents do with their children? Daycare. Sixty percent of all children age five or younger—13.3 million—are in some regular daycare arrangement, including half of all those under the age of two. Almost all children of employed mothers have some form of regular daycare, compared to one-fifth of children of nonemployed mothers.[7] Despite the warnings of researchers like Belsky and Barglow, daycare is—and probably will be for a long time—the lot of tens of millions of our nation's preschoolers.

How early does daycare begin for these children? Almost from birth for many of them. A Rand Corporation study finds that 38 percent of all women who become pregnant are in the workforce by the time their children are *three months old.* Among women who are employed during their pregnancy, 59 percent are back at work within three months of delivery.[8] It used to be that a woman's career was "interrupted" while she raised her children. No longer. If anything is interrupted, it's the mothering process.

HIGH RISK

Does this information trouble you? It does me. I'm not against women wanting or having careers. And I recognize that it costs

more than ever to live in our world today. But our society is playing a dangerous game that we cannot win by forcing or even
encouraging mothers into the work place. It was bad enough that
so many families lost their fathers to remote jobs in the cities following World War II. Now families are well on their way to losing
mothers, too. What sort of future marriages and families will these
combined losses produce?

Dr. Ken Magid and Carole McKelvey offer a chilling answer to
that question in their book entitled *High Risk: Children Without
Conscience*. They point out that it used to be the children of very
troubled homes who grew up to be anti-social, manipulative, and
without any ability to distinguish right from wrong. But more delin-
quents now come from so-called "normal homes," upper- and
middle-class families with law-abiding, hardworking parents. Why?

One key reason is that in their early, formative years, these
children fail to bond with any one caregiver. In the fast pace of life,
no one is really focused on them. As a result, they are "unattached"
emotionally. They have not learned to give or receive love in normal, healthy ways. Worst of all, they have no attachment to right
and wrong. They grow up without a sense of conscience, capable of
doing all kinds of vicious acts with no sense of regret or feeling.

We're in for a grim future with children growing up like that.
In fact, the future is already here. Danny Dawson of the Orange-
Osceola (Florida) County Juvenile Division was quoted as saying,
"Ten years ago it was a shock to see a seven-, eight-, or nine-year-
old come into the juvenile system. But now it's not. It's a trend."[9]

A shocking trend, but widespread: Florida police tried to
determine if a five-year-old knew the consequences of his actions
when he threw his three-year-old sibling off a fifth-floor stairwell.
Kansas City police were baffled by a jealous twelve-year-old who
killed his younger sister and mother over birthday party plans. A
teenage boy in Colorado waited patiently while two friends
hacked and hammered his mother to death.[10] And most of us have
heard of teenagers going on shooting rampages in their own
schools in quiet All-American cities like West Paducah, Kentucky,
and Springfield, Oregon. What's even more shocking is that none
of these children seems the least bit troubled by what they did.

With no conscience, it's "no big deal"!

Magid and McKelvey concluded:

> Our national spotlight should clearly be on the crib, not the criminal. Infants who do not receive a warm welcome into the world will seek their revenge.[11]

"How Do I Spell Working Mom? G-U-I-L-T!"

Critics will say that statistics and stories like these serve only to stir up needless fear and guilt among working mothers. No doubt they do. But are fear and guilt always "needless" and always to be avoided? Isn't it possible that sometimes they are appropriate reactions a mother should pay attention to? Couldn't her God-given maternal instincts be telling her something about the relative value of paid employment versus mothering? Needless or not, is she wise to ignore those feelings and concerns?

Obviously there are a growing number of mothers who really have no choice but to place their kids in daycare and head into the work world. Maybe they are widowed, divorced, or abandoned. Maybe their men are sick or disabled. Maybe they have no-account husbands who shirk their responsibilities. Whatever the reason, these women must take on the husband's role of providing in addition to their own role of mothering.

If you're a woman in this type of predicament and feel guilty for leaving your child while you work, I want to say that your guilt is indeed needless (though I know that doesn't take it away). You need to know that God is on your side. He stands with you in your time of need. He knows that you're doing double duty, and I believe He'll honor you for that. Your hard work to provide for your family is as much an expression of love and commitment as all of your maternal care.

Still, I don't want to back away from the fact that the single parent trying to do it all is not the family as God intended it. He certainly doesn't condemn single parenting. But He doesn't encourage it, either. It amazes me that many women who have responsible husbands earning a decent living, in effect, "single parent" their kids by placing them in daycare and going to work.

How well can such women fulfill their core role of nurturing the children God has given them?

Of course, many in our culture would prefer to skip over that question. Problem is, it won't go away, no matter how many magazine articles are written, speeches are made, and laws are passed. You see, our society has been conducting a giant social experiment over the past twenty or thirty years. In a radical break with the past, millions of mothers have left their children under the care of others in order to work outside the home. An entire daycare industry has sprung up to make this movement possible. A vast federal network of institutions is now being funded to replace Mom as the primary caregiver.

Now, after several decades of trial and error, new evidence is pouring in, and people are drawing sharply defined conclusions: "There is a clear perception among Americans that children are better off when the mother stays home and doesn't work," reported pollster George Gallup. Sixty-three percent of adults in the United States would prefer to have father working while mother stays home to care for children. One-half of working parents would want the mother to stay home "if money were not an issue." That feeling is even stronger among people in non-employed-mother households: 73 percent believe that children would be much better off with the mother at home[12]

Overall, there is a strong consensus that mothers should stay close to their little ones, if at all possible. One fifty-three-year-old mother of five grown children summarized the situation this way:

> We don't have a very good setup at present. Women have given up just being a mother and now they are expected to have a job, be the mother, the chauffeur and the nurse. Young women today are being cheated. And it's harder on the children when their mother works. People say it's quality time that counts, but if you have a full-time job, it's hard to have quality time with your children at the end of the day.[13]

No wonder a working mother with a two-year-old cries, "How do I spell working mom? G-u-i-l-t."[14] Millions of other women would spell it exactly the same way. Jonathan's mother would. Four-year-old Jonathan was asked by his preschool teacher, "What is love?" He answered sadly, "Love is slow."

The teacher felt his pain. The boy she had once known as lively and outgoing had gradually become quiet and withdrawn. So when Jonathan's mother arrived after work to pick him up, the teacher was waiting. She described what had happened. When she finished, the young mother burst into tears.

"I never have enough time," she said. "I rush him home from here and give him his supper and put him into bed and then I do the laundry and clean. In the morning *he is so slow;* and I nag him because I am afraid to be late for work. I never seem to have enough time to enjoy him the way I used to."[15]

LOVE IS SLOW

Does the above story break your heart? It does mine! Not just for Jonathan, but for his mother, too. Love *is* slow to a young child. It takes time—a lot of it—and large chunks of undivided attention. It just doesn't happen fast! So let's stop kidding ourselves. To a little one, love is a mother, and the strength behind a mother's love is the awesome power of being there—just being there! I believe she is divinely called and equipped for this purpose.

Love is slow. Nothing can change that for a child. The harder questions we must face are: Is love too slow to survive in our world? Is it too slow for today's woman? Is it too slow for you? No matter what you as a woman decide about working outside your home, I urge you not to neglect your core calling, that of loving your husband and your children. By being there for them, you are their greatest asset!

25

Seasons of Life

Ecclesiastes 3:1 (NIV) says, "There is a time for everything, and a season for every activity under heaven." The person who recorded that was called the wisest man who ever lived.[1] He affirmed that there is a time, a "season" for everything in life, including a season to work and a season to refrain from working.

God has designed seasons in a woman's life and family.
Employment is more appropriate in some seasons than others.

Extending the principle of seasons to the family, there are typically five seasons to parenting. Each one has its own opportunities, challenges, demands, and pleasures. Not surprisingly, the responsibilities change a bit as the seasons change. As her children grow up, her priorities shift and employment outside the home becomes more appropriate or less appropriate, depending on the season. Let's look, then, at these five typical seasons:

Just Married, No Children
The childless period may last less than a year. But many couples today are electing to start their families later in the marriage than

previous generations, so the childless period may last five years or more. One of the great blessings of this season is that the couple has a chance to get to know each other before little ones "invade" into the relationship.

Preschool Age Children
This is that beautiful season from the birth of a child to the beginning of formal schooling. Infancy. First steps. The acquisition of language. The sense of self. Endless questions. This is *the* crucial period in a child's development! Not only is much of his or her personality permanently established during this time, but an overall attitude toward life is fundamentally shaped.

Grade School Through High School Age Children
During this middle stage, the child socializes with the outside world and begins to acquire the skills needed to function in our society. The influence of teachers, coaches, and other mentors and authority figures comes into play. Values are formed. Relationships are built. The child begins to flex his or her independence in preparation for the next season—breaking away from home.

Young Adult Children
Our culture does not provide any formal rite of passage from childhood to adulthood. Consequently, this season often feels vague and undefined for both parents and child. The key element, though, is the need for the young adult to establish his or her own life, independent of the parents. This may happen through college, vocational school, military service, or a job.

The Empty Nest
This season arrives sooner than most couples realize. When their kids are in potty training, or later driving them crazy in adolescence, they long for the day when they can wave goodbye to Johnny or Susie. But when that day finally comes, the new "freedom" is not always as pleasant as the parents thought it would be. Now the husband and wife need to be reintroduced to each other and prepare their relationship for their later years. By the way,

adult children still need their parents during this season. And grandchildren will need grandparenting.

Obviously there is some overlap in these seasons, as children pass through the various stages. But any mother can see that children will demand more from her at some stages than at others; and therefore, outside employment is more appropriate during some seasons than others. The preschool years are especially demanding on a mother's time. So are the teenage years. And proper grandmothering takes a lot more time and energy than most women anticipate. The issue is not whether a woman should work during these seasons, but how well she can fulfill her core responsibilities.

SEASONS CHANGE

When Sherard and I were first married, I was excited about her job. She was a public school teacher working with mentally handicapped students in Portland's inner city. I was proud of her. She was an outstanding teacher, and the school system honored her for her fine work. But in time there came a different season in our life together. God blessed us with children—four of them. So now Sherard devotes herself to being a "child-lover" to them. They need more attention than either of us ever imagined on the front end. But that won't be the case forever. Before long they'll be grown up and independent, and Sherard will enter a new season once again.

Who knows what things she'll pursue in that new season? She'll certainly have a lot more time for things outside the home. Maybe she'll return to the teaching profession, or pursue some special ministry she feels drawn to. Whatever the next season may bring, I feel confident that she'll use her gifts and abilities in special ways. Yet even then, I hope that she'll never violate her core role with respect to me, just as I hope never to violate my core role with respect to her.

Seasons change, and Ecclesiastes 3:11 (NIV) goes on to say, "[God] has made everything beautiful in its time." Every season has its own beauty, its own value. A wise woman knows that. She possesses a "big picture" view of life. She anticipates each season and what it offers and orders the years of her life by that long-term perspective.

QUESTIONS TO ASK

Before we leave the issue of employed mothers, I want to stress again how complex it is. There is no one, simple answer that fits every woman's situation. As a woman, you need to evaluate the needs of your family, as well as your own needs. You need to discuss them with your husband, and even with your children. You need to reflect carefully on the principles I've focused on in these last three chapters: (1) God expects you to fulfill your core role, whether or not you go to work; (2) providing for your family's basic financial needs is your husband's role, not yours; and (3) employment is more appropriate during some seasons in your family's life than others.

In addition, I encourage you to ask yourself the following questions about outside employment. In fact, writing down your answers is one way to clarify your thoughts.

1. Am I attempting to meet my needs, fulfill my life, and find my significance through a career or through my relationship with God? What is the source of my identity and sense of worth?

2. As a wife, where is my primary focus? Is my concentration devoted to things outside my home, or on the dynamics of my family?

3. Do my husband and children receive the love and attention from me that they need? How does (or would) my employment affect that?

4. What is my reason for working outside the home (or considering it)? Is it a *need* or a *want?*

5. Do I feel forced to have a job? What is the source of this pressure?

6. Is my husband in agreement with my employment? Are we united on this point?

7. Someday my kids and I will look back on my decision to work outside the home. What might they say about it? What will I say?

There are no "right" answers to these questions—just the answers you supply. But questions like these will not go away. By reflecting on them carefully, you can discover a lot about yourself and your motives regarding work outside the home.

STRATEGIES FOR WORKING WOMEN

Of course, I'm aware that most women reading this book are either already in the work place or else will be at some point in the next few years. Many couples would prefer that the wife not work, at least not before their children are a certain age. Others know the wife must work; still, they want to minimize any negative impact on their families.

Here are six suggestions for couples to consider:

1. *Save money early in your marriage.* When you are in the first season — just married, no children — learn to live *solely* on the husband's income. If the wife has a job, put her paycheck in savings or a secure investment account. Trust me, you'll need that money later! Better to have it in hand than to have to work for it all over again.
2. *Plan your family.* I'm amazed at couples who sign up for house payments, car payments, and the like — based on two incomes—*then* start their families. I question what kind of planning has led to that because it virtually guarantees that the wife must work and that there will be a lot of stress.
3. *Avoid debt.* You've heard it before! This is *the number-one trap* that young couples fall into. Debt means living today on tomorrow's dollars, ensuring that a husband and wife will have to go out and find those dollars. It also means that when tomorrow comes, the money you are making will already be spoken for — at the very time you need it for a growing family! If as a couple you want the wife to avoid employment, or at least work less, pay cash, live simply, and *stay out of debt!*
4. *Evaluate whether part-time or full-time work is more suited to the wife's needs.* There's no simple answer here. My point is that if the wife needs to work, make sure the amount of work taken on meets your needs (and no more). The issue is efficiency. Some women who work part-time

are wasting energy because the money and benefits *after* expenses don't really meet the need that put them to work in the first place. On the other hand, some women are working full-time, to the detriment of their families, when a similar job part-time could work just as well.

5. *Consider working out of your home.* This is a growing trend for men as well as women, and I welcome it. For some people and some kinds of work, it can be an ideal way to balance work and family. Are you that kind of person? Is your home suited to the kind of work you do? If you do work out of your home, give yourself a chance to succeed by setting up a well-defined work space, setting regular hours, getting the right tools, and so on.

6. *Set and enforce boundaries with your employer and customers.* The days when employers could expect slave-like devotion from their employees are on the way out. But you still need to be clear and firm about your limits, needs, and requirements. These have to do with such things as your hours; whether or not (or how much) you will travel; advance notice for overtime or unusual assignments; the amount of responsibility you can handle; business calls to and from your home; sick days; and the like. Without question you want to be a professional and praiseworthy employee. But to remain effective, you also have to be effective in your role with your family. Only *you* know how to strike that balance.

THE SECRET OF A WIFE'S SUCCESS

Let's go back again to Proverbs 31. Many people feel that this passage portrays the "ideal" Hebrew wife. Some see in her an industrious businesswoman whose shrewd dealings help support her family. On that basis they encourage today's women to join their husbands in the workforce and help earn a living for their families. Others, however, find her solely devoted to domestic responsibilities, and therefore a model for today's career homemaker. Still others see her somewhere in between.

However you choose to see her, the Proverbs 31 woman

deserves attention because she manages to earn the praise of her husband, her children, her community, and ultimately the Lord. What woman would not want that? Verse 30 tells us the secret of her success:

> Charm is deceitful and beauty is vain,
> But a woman who fears the Lord, she shall be praised.

Charm and beauty have historically been used as measures of a woman's worth. Today we might add career success to these. But Scripture insists that these external assets are "vain"—literally, empty or fleeting, *of no lasting value.* What ultimately matters is whether a woman fears the Lord. That is, does she live her life on the basis of God's principles and priorities? Are her choices conditioned by His approval? Or does she follow the prevailing culture, swept up in society's agenda for women, without regard for God's perspective?

As a wife you may or may not choose employment outside the home. Either way, I challenge you to make a healthy fear of the Lord the operating principle for your life. According to Proverbs 31, that's the way to win lasting praise from those who matter most to you (verses 28-29):

> Her children rise up and bless her;
> Her husband also, and he praises her, saying:
> "Many daughters have done nobly,
> But you excel them all."

26

Gifting Your Child's Marriage

Writing in the *Stanford University Observer,* Dr. Albert Seigel warned:

> When it comes to rearing children, every society is only twenty years away from barbarism. Twenty years is all we have to accomplish the task of civilizing the infants who are born into our midst each year. The infant is totally ignorant about democracy and civil liberties, respect, decency, honesty, customs, conventions and all manners. The Barbarian must be tamed if civilization is to survive.[1]

Assuming that Dr. Seigel is correct, what sort of society will we have in twenty years? It is sobering to realize that tomorrow's marriages are being forged right now in today's homes. Dr. Peter Blitchington, in his book *Sex Roles and the Christian Family,* concurred: "Parents . . . shape a child's personality and give him most of the advantages (or disadvantages) that he will enjoy in later years."[2] I don't know about you, but that scares the daylights out of me! Especially when I think about my own deficiencies and my own selfishness. I realize that in ways known and unknown I pass these on to my kids.

CULTURE IN CRISIS

I'm even more troubled when I look at all the casualties our society is propagating: "Every year, more than 1 million children under 18 watch their parents divorce."[3]

An unprecedented long-term study of the effects of divorce found that:

Half of children of divorces enter adulthood as worried, under-achieving, self-deprecating and sometimes angry young men and women.

Three out of five youngsters of divorce felt rejected by at least one parent.

Two-thirds of the girls became deeply anxious as young adults, unable to make lasting commitments and fearful of betrayal in intimate relationships.

Many of the boys failed to develop a sense of independence, confidence or purpose. They drifted in and out of college and from job to job.[4]

By the year 2000, more than half of all children will spend part of their lives in a single-parent home.[5]

As chilling as these statistics are, they represent only the tip of the iceberg. A more troubling question is, "How healthy are the homes that are not torn by divorce?" As a pastor with twenty years of experience, my answer is: not very healthy! Tomorrow's marriages will experience even greater suffering because of the deficiencies children are acquiring in many of today's homes.

THE "ME GENERATION" AND THE MODERN MARRIAGE

How did things in the United States get the way they are? Well, following Dr. Seigel's lead, let's look back twenty years. We were just emerging from the 1960s. If ever there was a time when our entire way of life was called into question and every institution was condemned, it was the sixties. People like Abbie Hoffman and Jerry Rubin were the social heroes of the day. Young people called for virtual anarchy, throwing accepted standards, customs, convictions, and morals to the wind. Writer Tom Wolfe dubbed these young upstarts the "Me Generation," a group of affluent kids pre-occupied with self-fulfillment.

That was the sixties. Here we are, twenty years later. That same sixties generation has produced the marriages of today. And while I wouldn't describe our culture with Seigel's term as "barbaric," I do think it is worth asking: Are today's marriages better off than the marriages of the preceding generation? Are today's couples, having come out of a self-indulgent, me-first society, better at making marriages work than their parents were? Have the building blocks of free love, the repudiation of marriage roles, the masculinization of women, the emphasis on personal rights, and the pursuit of pleasure and self-gain constructed solid, lasting marriages?

Obviously not. The anarchy and selfishness of the sixties has only disadvantaged marriages in the eighties and nineties. In large measure, yesterday's confusion has raised today's chaos. Yesterday's sexual promiscuity has produced today's sexual confusion and perversion. Yesterday's rebellion has birthed today's violence.

The sixties put many of today's marriages at a serious disadvantage. But things will be even worse in the next twenty years if you and I fail to prepare our children appropriately. If we do fail, I fear for them, and frankly, I fear for the survival of our nation.

As Christians, we can't afford to take our parental responsibilities lightly. We must embrace them radically. We must give our children a solid understanding of what it means to be a man or a woman; an understanding of the opposite sex; clarity as to what role they should assume in marriage; and most importantly, how that role is to be implemented and lived out. An anonymously written poem says it well:

I saw tomorrow marching
on little children's feet.
Within their forms and faces
her prophecy now complete.
I saw tomorrow look at me
from little children's eyes

and thought—how carefully we would teach
if we were really wise.[6]

GIFTED CHILDREN

Whether tomorrow's marriages will be solid and satisfying for our children depends on two things. First, God's grace. Thank God that He can help people overcome the mistakes of their parents. That is grace. And it has saved many. Second, it also depends on our diligence as parents to "gift" tomorrow's generation.

Usually when we think of giftedness we think of gifted children—young people blessed with an unusually high degree of intelligence, beauty, or athletic prowess. In our secular world, these are the ultimate gifts of life. But the Bible describes giftedness much differently.

For instance, a gifted child from the biblical perspective is one with a high and lofty sense of his or her identity. She knows what it means to be forgiven from sin. He knows what grace is all about. She knows what Christlike love and unconditional acceptance mean, and she carries her head high because she is an eternal child of God. A gifted child from the biblical perspective has a well-defined set of values and a crystal clear sense of right and wrong.

A gifted child in the biblical sense has a solid work ethic, too. He understands that work is not a curse, nor is it an avenue for self-ishness; rather, work is an honorable gift from God to be used in serving others. A gifted child has a sense of mission—in the words of the *Westminster Catechism,* "to glorify God and enjoy Him forever." Finally, she has a solid sense of what a biblical marriage is all about and appreciates the roles that God has given her and her husband. That's a gifted child from a biblical point of view.

So how can we endow our children with these gifts? I think we find direction in Ephesians 6:4:

> Fathers, do not provoke your children to anger; but bring
> them up in the discipline and instruction of the Lord.

This exhortation, like so many others in Scripture, singles out fathers. Obviously both parents must be involved in child-rearing. But fathers bear the ultimate responsibility to see that their children are brought up in the manner indicated. And the truth is, fathers tend to struggle with this issue far more than mothers. Notice the word *but*. It sets up a profound contrast. On one side is the discipline and instruction of the Lord; on the other is anger. *Either* teach children *or* provoke them. Which will it be?

This may seem an unusual contrast at first glance. Yet, it's clear to me why Paul set this verse up in the way he did. The angriest kids I know are the ones who grow up without direction, without instruction, without limits — all of which are to be endowed by loving parents. These kids come out angry because deep down they feel aimless, incompetent, and out of control. They've never had anyone show them how to live.

THE ANGER OF INCOMPETENCE

I can identify deeply with those feelings because that's the way I was raised. My father was a quiet and socially withdrawn man. To a large extent, he was removed from the lives of his children. I called him The Shadow. He did little in the way of preparing us for life. So I grew up deficient in many of the basic how-to's that fathers are supposed to pass on to their sons. In time, that void began to surface, and when it did, it created a tremendous anger within me.

I remember standing around with my buddies, talking about car engines. They all knew what a cylinder was, and how to change the oil, and what a spark plug did and how to gap it. But I didn't. I felt odd, stupid. And it made me mad. When we went fishing, my friends knew how to tie the hook on the line and what baits to use and where to fish. But I didn't. I would get teased for my incompetence. It hurt — and inside it made me mad. There were times we would play basketball. Everyone seemed to know the rules, knew how to dribble and pass and shoot, and had the right equipment. They had learned these things from their dads. These skills were just part of a knowledge base that they assumed every boy had.

But I didn't have them. So when they saw me struggling, they gave me jokes and jabs, as boys will do. I often left feeling humiliated. Let me tell you, it was tough learning everything from the school of hard knocks. It gets old. I got angry.

This incompetency extended into my teenage years to my relationships with the opposite sex. Even children who have been shown the practical how-to's may not have been taught any social how-to's. As a result, I had no idea how to act around a girl. I had no understanding of what a girl is really like, how she thinks or what she feels. My perception of women was gathered mostly from shallow cliches, media images, and sexual myths. As a result, I made a lot of mistakes that cost me a lot of pain. It was infuriating. This is what I call "the anger of incompetence."

Today, I know a lot of young couples who are frustrated with each other and their marriage because neither partner knows how to correctly relate to the opposite sex. Nobody has ever told them. They are trying to build an intimate relationship, one that's supposed to last a lifetime, from scratch or, at best, guesswork. That can be maddening, and it often erupts in violence as the newspapers report every day. These young people don't realize that *behind much of their quarrels and dysfunction and anger is what they don't know,* not *who they're married to.* They were never taught the basics. Now they're operating out of that ignorance. They've been given no resources, no gifting, no advantages to draw on.

Ephesians 6 tells us as parents: You can either teach your children how to live, or you can doom them to a lifetime of frustration and anger. Practical biblical instruction on marriage while your children are still at home can go a long way toward alleviating a plethora of unnecessary hurt in later life.

FOUR OBJECTIVES

If you want to gift your children for their future marriages, let me suggest you pursue four objectives. Sherard and I are trying to cultivate these in our own kids:

1. Equip them with practical insights concerning the differences between men and women. Help them see that there is blessing and power in two points of view.
2. Teach them to be aware of the special needs men and

women have and how to meet those needs in practical
ways.

3. Give them a solid understanding of what their biblical role
is to be in marriage.

4. Let them know how impossible all this is apart from the
Holy Spirit assisting and helping them.

These are four wonderful assets no child should leave home
without. They are also "anger-busters."

Of course, the transference of these kinds of competencies
cannot be done by the lips alone. To truly "gift" our children for
tomorrow's marriages, *we parents must connect the teaching that
comes off our lips with the lifestyle we live out.*

In 1 Timothy 4, Paul tells Timothy that this "connection" in
his own life would be vital to those under his care (verse 16):

> Pay close attention to yourself and to your teaching; perse-
> vere in these things; for as you do this you will insure salva-
> tion both for yourself and for those who hear you.

Paul says that good modeling from a spiritual leader can *save* a
congregation from the confusion that mixed signals give and the
hurt that follows. If that's true for a church, it's also true for a home.
Good modeling from a parent can save children, too. You can
empower your children's future when they hear instruction from
your lips and then see it replayed in your life. That kind of clarity
can save them from all kinds of unnecessary hurt.

You Leave What You Live

Remember Lot in Genesis 19? The New Testament describes Lot
as "righteous," meaning he was a God-fearer, a believer.[7] But Lot
also was a man whose life contradicted his belief. He compro-
mised himself for the prosperity around Sodom and Gomorrah,
despite the wickedness that filled those towns. He moved his family there, and before long they were living the same evil lifestyle.
One day two angels appeared to Lot, saying that God was about to
destroy those cities. Immediately Lot went to warn his family.

Perhaps for the first time in his life, he sought to exercise some real spiritual leadership (Genesis 19:14, emphasis added):

> Lot went out and spoke to his sons-in-law . . . and said, "Up, get out of this place, for the Lord will destroy the city." But *he appeared to his sons-in-law to be jesting.*

Imagine this, if you will. In the moment of crisis, Lot was desperately trying to save his family. No doubt he used religious words such as *sin, judgment,* and *evil.* But Lot's spiritual credibility was already shot. So much so that his children dismissed him as playing a joke. "Come on, Dad! God condemn us? Stop kidding. We haven't done anything wrong. What's wrong? What's right? Very funny, Dad!"

Why did Lot receive this response? Because of the great gulf between his beliefs and his lifestyle.

You will leave in your children what you have lived out in your home. You can leave a gift or a joke. Certainly, it depends on what you teach, but even more on how you live. This poem provides a good model:

> *I'd rather see a sermon*
> *than hear one any day.*
> *I'd rather one should walk with me*
> *than merely show the way.*
> *The eye's a better pupil*
> *and more willing than the ear.*
> *Fine counsel can be confusing,*
> *but example is always clear.*
> *For I might misunderstand you*
> *and the high advice you give,*
> *but there is no misunderstanding*
> *in how you act and how you live.*[8]
> —Anonymous

What example are you showing your kids that will gift their marriages twenty years from now? Will they be advantaged because of the legacy you have left? Will your sons be servant-leaders to their wives? Will they be able to pass on a godly heritage to their children—your grandchildren? Will your daughters know how to love their husbands and their children? Will they be able to nurture them as only a woman can?

You see, this is the most significant legacy you'll leave on this planet. What you leave in your estate, what you accomplish in your career, what you do for your community, even the help you give to your church—none of these will have quite as powerful an impact, or make a more poignant statement about your own character, as the children you send out into the world. And before you go, nothing will compare with the satisfaction of watching your children live out that legacy, if it's a good one. That's what Proverbs 23:24-25 says:

> The father of the righteous will greatly rejoice,
> And he who begets a wise son will be glad in him.
> Let your father and your mother be glad,
> And let her rejoice who gave birth to you.

On the other hand, Proverbs 17:21,25 describes the tragedy of raising a child who throws his or her life away:

> He who begets a fool does so to his sorrow,
> And the father of a fool has no joy. . . .
> A foolish son is a grief to his father,
> And bitterness to her who bore him.

The future happiness of your children largely depends on the spiritual, moral, and personal gifts that you give them today. Your own sense of joy and satisfaction depend on it as well.

A Tragedy in the Making

In 1949, actress Mercedes McCambridge won an Academy Award. I'm sure she felt on top of the world. Certainly she was at the top of her career. The whole industry applauded what she had accomplished on film.

But her son, John, didn't join the party. To the outside world, the McCambridge home glittered. But for a son who needed a mother, this family was anything but a success. Even though John later became a very successful financial broker, his life was haunted by the deficits his upbringing had left within him. In the spring of 1989, he exploded. Before murdering his own wife and two children and then committing suicide, he penned these words to his famous mother:

> I was essentially raised by live-in maids and relatives. You never were there for me. I tried to get your love through academic achievement, gifts, and, finally, enormous personal risk. You love to tell the story of the boy who got paid to babysit himself. That means I was left alone. Alone! At five years old, in his little suit and hat, flying across the country alone. Alone! Is this clear to you, mom? . . . There is nothing more to say.[9]

You will leave in your children what you have lived out in your home. Can you imagine the horror and heartbreak that this young man's mother must have felt? Yet his tragic outcome was forged long ago. His wings were clipped long before he got married. Though highly gifted with intelligence, he obviously grew up without emotional stability.

I'm not suggesting that if you fail as a parent your children will grow up to commit murder-suicides. But we need to wake up and see that the growing sickness of our society can in large measure be traced to homes where children are entertained, not *loved;* educated, but not *gifted;* kept busy, but not carefully *mentored.*

Perhaps hearing this story troubles you because you feel like you've already blown it with your kids. If so, let me encourage you that it's never too late to start reclaiming lost ground. It's never too late to start turning your own life around and, in the process, impacting your children in some positive and powerful ways. By all means, ask God to help you and trust that He will.

Would you like to give your children the ultimate wedding gift? Then start gifting their marriage of tomorrow—today!

27

New Life
for Your Marriage!

During the Persian Gulf War, the television networks showed countless scenes of parched, empty wastes in Saudi Arabia and surrounding areas. One look at those barren lands and you could tell that no creature could last for long if abandoned on those trackless sands.

The best illustration of that truth and all I've been saying is found in Ezekiel 37. In that passage, a great prophecy is presented about the restoration of Israel. The nation is scattered and the people are despondent. They live under the crushing might of a wicked foreign power—Babylon, distant ancestor to modern-day Iraq.

Ezekiel envisioned his people as a valley full of dead, dry bones. Listen:

> The hand of the Lord was upon me, and He brought me out by the Spirit of the Lord and set me down in the middle of the valley; and it was full of bones. And He caused me to pass among them round about, and behold, there were very many . . . ; and lo, they were very dry. And He said to me, "Son of man, can these bones live?" (Ezekiel 37:1-3)

God then told Ezekiel to prophesy two things to this lifeless scene. First, Ezekiel exhorted the scattered bones to hear God's word of hope and renewal. As he did this, the dry bones began to move:

> As I prophesied, there was a noise, and behold, a rattling; and the bones came together, bone to its bone. (verse 7)

Immediately, after the skeletons were completed, they were filled and covered with flesh.

Then Ezekiel prophesied a second time. But this prophecy was directed to the "breath," not the bones. *Breath* is a word synonymous with the Spirit of God:

> So I prophesied as He commanded me, and the breath [Spirit] came into them [the bones], and they came to life, and stood on their feet, an exceedingly great army. (verse 10)

The scene was totally transformed—from lifeless dry bones, to a nation of people full of life. This was the picture of revival God offered to a despondent, beaten nation.

I believe it is also a wonderful and accurate outline of revival for today's dry marriages. Perhaps your relationship has died, leaving nothing but dry bones scattered about. It may be as hopeless as a desiccated skeleton lying in the Arabian desert. You're wondering, *How can these bones ever come to life? How can my marriage ever live again?* The first thing Ezekiel would say is, "Hear the word of the Lord!" Hearing God's Word is the first step to bringing dry marriages together again.

As I pastor, I've seen countless couples who were headed for divorce come into the church, sometimes as a last resort. They begin to hear preaching and teaching that challenges them with godly principles of marriage. And you know what? Their relationship begins to change! They stop blaming and start listening to each other. There's hope. There's direction. Instead of fighting and thinking about how they can end their relationship, they start thinking about how they can come back together and make it work. God's Word is that powerful. And it's wonderful. Yet that in itself is not enough!

They need Ezekiel's second prophecy. The dry bones of their

marriage have come together, but they're still just dry, dead bones. You see, rules and principles, as important as they are, are not enough to make a relationship live. Even though a couple commits to following the biblical blueprints on marriage—the husband says, "I need to be a servant-leader in my family," and the wife says, "I need to support and nurture my husband and children"— that alone won't cause the relationship to "come alive" because, in the flesh, a husband or wife is not able to consistently live that way. They need more than God's Word.

It takes the Spirit of God to get a marriage on its feet! Only *in Him* can a marriage really live. That's why Ezekiel makes a second prophecy in which the Spirit breathes His life into these lifeless bodies. And so it is in your marriage. You need the Spirit to breathe life into your marriage every day, to empower you to be the husband or wife described in Scripture. It's great to study the Word of God, and you must do that if you want the Spirit to minister to you. But Bible knowledge alone will not make your marriage live. Only the Spirit can do that. Only He can rescue you from "Dry Bones Valley."

That's why the greatest help I can recommend to you is the Holy Spirit. In this book I've given a lot of information based on Scripture. Study it. Master what the Bible says about marriage. You can trust its clear, proven directives. But don't stop there! Each day ask the Spirit for help to live out this truth in your relationship. He's there beside you, even though you can't see Him. Why not take a moment right now to pray something like this:

Holy Spirit, come and fill my marriage with the life it needs. Teach me truth in the crucial moments of my marriage. Empower me to respond to my partner the way that I should. Take these dry bones of our relationship and breathe life into them so that our marriage becomes a union as beautiful and pure as Christ's is with His Church. Amen.

FOR DISCUSSION

1. Wives, have you ever struggled with the decision of whether or not to work outside the home? Why—what was the point of struggle? Read Hebrews 13:5 and 1 Timothy 6:8. What do these verses say in light of society's push to have more and do more?

2. Of course, some couples realize after having children that the wife *must* work outside the home, even though she would rather stay home with the children. If you find yourself in this situation, reread the questions in chapter 25 under the subhead "Questions to Ask." Wives, answer these questions for yourself; ask your husband to answer them about you. Discuss your answers. If you *must* work, your attitude about your core role as a wife and mom can make a big difference in the way you feel about working and about your family.

3. Read Proverbs 31:10-30. List the different work-related things the woman in this passage did. Discuss how she could be a godly woman as well as being a working woman.

4. Do you think it's important to leave a strong marriage "legacy" for your children? As a couple, discuss how you can strengthen the message you're sending to your kids about marriage and its roles. What could you do better? For a real treat, ask your kids what they think about your marriage. Their answers might surprise you!

5. Read the "Four Objectives" in chapter 26. Discuss how you're doing in teaching each of these areas to your children. Read 1 Timothy 4:16. What do you think this verse is saying about how you teach others—including your children?

6. Husbands, pray for your wife that she will understand and enjoy the beautiful role of helper-lover that God created her to fulfill. Pray that she'll know an abundance of satisfaction for fulfilling that role. Likewise, wives pray for your husband that he will desire to fulfill the wonderful role of servant-leader God created him to fulfill. Pray that he'll understand that nothing is more important to you or your children than fulfilling that role. God bless both of you!

APPENDIX

I.

Roleless Chaos of Another Day

Our day is one of incredible change. Society is undergoing a fundamental shift in relations between the sexes. We are rapidly breaking with the past as the nature of marriage evolves. Couples everywhere are struggling to sort it all out. Do you ever long wistfully for a return to simpler times, when things seemed less complex and more stable? You're not alone!

> In the good old days, in fact right down to recent years, married women ran their homes as their chief domain. Their husbands would come home at night and plop themselves down by the fireside, lay their cares aside, and rest from their busy day out in the world. Without question the men were in charge; yet an atmosphere of harmony and hard work prevailed under their roofs. It was a day when their wives — beautiful women — burned only with the desire to make their men all that they could be, especially in business. This division of labor was never territorial; neither partner laid claim to ownership of anything. Rather, they cooperated for the good of the family: she worked as diligently at home as he did in his public activities. . . .

Nowadays, though, it seems as though women only want to pursue material gain. They want to be rid of even the most basic household responsibilities, as if to become nothing but consumers of luxury items, often bankrupting their families in the process.[1]

Another observer lamented the effect this change has had on children:

There used to be a time when an honest child was raised, not at the hand of some hired nurse, but in his mother's lap, and at her knee. In those days a mother could have no higher praise than that she managed her house well and gave herself to her children. Of course, she had plenty of help: when occupied elsewhere, she could call upon a trustworthy grandmother to care for all the little saplings taking root in her home. She knew that the elder would not stand for any foul language or misbehavior. Religiously, and with the utmost delicacy, the older lady would oversee not only the serious tasks of her young charges, but also their games and play.

Nowadays, by contrast, too many children are handed over almost from birth to some daycare worker, who might let just anyone assist her—quite often the least-qualified sort of person. These people take no thought of the kind of conversation they have, giving children their earliest impressions of the world, while their minds are still green and unformed. It's a disgrace, really, that parents could care so little about what these caretakers say in front of their children. Even worse, the parents themselves make no effort to train their little ones in goodness and self-control. As a result, children grow up in an atmosphere of laxity and poor manners. Over time they come to lose all sense of shame and all respect, both for themselves and for other people.[2]

THE MORE THINGS CHANGE . . .

These writers sound a lot like people I know. By the way, did I mention that they were writing 2,000 years ago? The authors,

Columella and Tacitus, were two Romans of the first century—
the very period when Christ and His apostles launched the Church
and spread the gospel message throughout the Roman Empire.

I present these loose paraphrases of their remarks to show that
the world in which Christianity took root was far more like our
own than most people realize. When Paul wrote that wives were to
be "subject to their own husbands" (Ephesians 5:24) and "workers
at home" (Titus 2:5), and that the husband was the "head" of the
wife (Ephesians 5:23), his words probably sounded as out-of-
place then as they do today. Yet he boldly proclaimed God's message anyway.

That message emerged during a time of extraordinary cultural
change. The old Roman republic had collapsed in 27 B.C. when
Octavian took control and proclaimed himself emperor, Caesar
Augustus.[3] This change of government had a profound and lasting
effect on life throughout the Empire.

For instance, it brought a general peace in which cities flour-
ished. Many people think of the Bible as a rural book. But much of
the New Testament was written to people in urban settings, many
of which were as sophisticated and cosmopolitan as any metropolis today. Wide-ranging trade and commerce took hold as a mone-
tary-based economy gradually replaced the old barter methods.
Systems of transportation and communication brought together
peoples from extraordinarily diverse cultural backgrounds.[4]

By way of comparison, think about similar changes in our own
time: the major shift from rural to urban areas; the ever-expanding
influence of our own federal government; the rise of a global economy; the collapse of the Eastern bloc alliance and the emergence of
the European Economic Community; the construction of a global
network of telephones, computers, and satellites. Consider the profound impact that these and other developments have on you and
your family. In ways known and unknown they affect your job,
your income, your purchases, and your plans. They affect your values and world-view. They affect your relationships, too.

Changes in the first-century Roman world had their most dramatic impact on social life. Families had to contend with many of
the same issues, stresses, and problems that you and I face. As in

our society, their marriages failed at an alarming rate, and family life unraveled despite increasing prosperity. Most fascinating, perhaps, is the fact that, like us, Roman couples looked back on an idealized view of the family that supposedly existed in its past (the one Columella and Tacitus praised), with Dad out in the world earning a living, and Mom at home overseeing kids and servants. Sound familiar?

The first century even had its own version of Donna Reed. We know from thousands of surviving gravestone inscriptions about her virtues: she was old-fashioned (*antiqua vita*); content to stay at home (*domiseda*); chaste (*pudicitia*); dutifully obedient (*obsequiem*); friendly and amusing (*comitas, sermone lepido*); careful over money (*frugi*); not over-dressed (*ornatus non conspiciendi*); religious without being fanatical (*religionis sine superstitione*); and above all, adept at spinning and weaving (*lanifica, lanam fecit*).[5]

FIRST-CENTURY WOMEN

Such was the image of the first-century ideal. But what was the reality? It would be difficult if not impossible to say with absolute certainty.[6] We do know that by the time of Augustus, the famous patriarchal Roman family that had dominated the days when Rome was a republic, before the Empire, was in sharp decline. Despite laws on the books that made men sovereign over their wives and children, the social order of the day was far different. "Legislation kept women subject, custom made them free."[7] Indeed, "It is certain that the Roman woman . . . enjoyed a dignity and an independence at least equal if not superior to those claimed by contemporary feminists."[8]

Far from being "cooped up" at home, we find Roman women engaged in a wide variety of occupations, some with their husbands, many on their own.[9] Freedwomen (female slaves set free) "comprised a large part of the Roman working class, serving as shopkeepers or artisans or continuing in domestic service." As women had always been the ones to work in wool, they monopolized Rome's textile manufacturing,[10] including the widespread trade in purple, an expensive cloth dyed from the extract of a certain clamshell.[11]

Women sold perfume, ran laundries, worked at mills where grain was ground, managed real estate, and lent money. They sold clothing and food, and worked as butchers and even fisherwomen. Many worked as waitresses in taverns and at counters dispensing food and drinks. Others became prostitutes—a legal, taxable trade recognized by some as a respectable investment. Some were known for their simple occupations—"dealer in beans" or "seller of nails"—others for their professional roles as commercial entrepreneurs, physicians, and lawyers.

Their names are stamped on pipes and bricks, indicating involvement in construction, perhaps as the owner of a brick-making or stone-cutting operation, or as a laborer in the making of building materials or construction work itself. So many were employed in shipbuilding that the emperor Claudius offered them special rewards to assist him in his naval program.[12]

THE COLLAPSE OF THE ROMAN FAMILY

Viewed from our perspective two millennia later, these opportunities for women look positive and progressive. Compared to most other ancient cultures, they were. But it is worth noting that this trend away from home paralleled a massive tide of moral and social decline that hit the Empire just before Christianity arrived on the scene. The institution of marriage, once a lifelong union, "was now among a hundred thousand Romans a passing adventure of no great spiritual significance."[13] Divorce became the normal course of affairs.[14] Sound familiar?

To counter the trend, Augustus passed numerous laws concerning marriage, divorce, childbirth, and inheritance. He wanted to revive family priorities. But his statutes did little good. "From this time on we witness an epidemic of divorces—at least among the aristocracy whose matrimonial adventures are documented—and in spite of the laws of Augustus, or perhaps rather on account of them, the disease tended to become endemic under the Empire."[15] Seneca, a philosopher of the day, chided Roman women by remarking, "They divorce in order to remarry. They marry in order to divorce."[16]

Adultery became the accepted and expected norm for both

husbands and wives.[17] "Pure women," sang the cynical Ovid, "are only those who have not been asked; and a man who is angry at his wife's amours is a mere rustic." Seneca's philosopher-son defined a faithful married woman as one who had only two lovers.[18] In a satire by Juvenal, an unfaithful wife is discovered by her husband; she then reminds him, "We agreed long ago that you were to go your way and I mine. You may confound sea and sky with your bellowing. I am a human being after all."[19] Sound familiar?

The remark would make a great sound-bite for "Entertainment Tonight"! It sounds so contemporary and Madonna-like—defiant, autonomous, self-indulgent. We can't say that *all* Roman women held such a view. But the attitude was widespread among the upper classes, especially those in large cities, and it helped to undermine the institution of marriage.

We know that one of the fundamental causes of Rome's decline was a drop in the birth rate. Many explanations have been suggested for this. Of course, the men of that day blamed the women for evading home duties:

> The refusal of women to assume the burdens and conse-
> quences of motherhood, the first of their responsibilities, was
> identified as a cause for the drop in births. Always greedier
> for pleasures and luxury, women were seen as the cause of
> irreparable imbalance of payments. Silks had to be imported
> from China; perfumes came from Arabia; jewels from the
> Orient. Tiberius [who ruled from A.D. 14–37 as Augustus'
> successor] . . . claimed that the extravagance of women had
> enriched Rome's enemies while impoverishing the Romans.[20]

Doubtless the men were overlooking complex economic, financial, sociological, and military factors, many of which they had created. And they failed to mention their own greed, selfishness, and irresponsibility. Still, you can feel from their words that the social fabric of Roman society was unraveling. Motherhood was devalued; as a result, the Empire was unable to replenish its armies and supply enough new business and political leaders.

Augustus became so concerned that he actually imposed a tax

on women who married and tried to remain childless. If, on the other hand, a mother bore more than three children, she earned a federal subsidy, and her husband no longer had any power over her. She was even given a cloak to distinguish her among the people. Especially fertile women were publicly exhibited at events such as the gladiatorial games in Rome. Augustus invited them to sit in his private box, honoring them for their service on Rome's behalf.[21]

Whatever impression these efforts made on the crowds, they failed to increase the birthrate. A significant number of upper-class women simply refused to have children. Some married eunuchs so as to lay sole claim to their husbands' estates. Others negotiated before marriage that they needn't bear children and might have as many lovers as they pleased.[22]

Abortion and infanticide were common.[23] "Philosophers and the law condemned it, but the finest families practiced it. 'Poor women,' says Juvenal, 'endure the perils of childbirth, and all the troubles of nursing . . . but how often does a gilded bed harbor a pregnant woman? So great is the skill, so powerful the drugs, of the abortionist!'"[24] Sound familiar?

A Repeat of History?

I offer this glimpse of first-century Rome for a very important reason: Our own society appears to be headed in the same direction. Historians will forever argue over what caused the decline and fall of Rome. Whether it was primarily the result of the breakdown of the Roman family is beside the point. The real lesson here is that a society of unstable families is a society in trouble. It's like a ship without a keel, reeling from one crisis to the next.

Such was the case in Rome. For all its glory and might, the Empire was collapsing from within, morally exhausted and spiritually bankrupt. The telltale sign that its end was near was the loss of its family structure, the basic building block of society.

Which way is the wind blowing in our own culture? We know that more than half of all new marriages today end in divorce. At that rate, married couples will be a minority of households by 2010.[25] More than one million children each year see their parents split up.[26] Already, one out of four lives with only one parent.[27]

I could fill a book with statistics like these. But the point is made: Something is wrong with the American family. And if Roman history is any guide, that means something is terribly wrong with the United States.

Yet we're foolish to simply wring our hands and say that nothing can be done. For at the very time when Roman family life was at its worst, God intervened (Luke 2:1):

> It came about in those days that a decree went out from Caesar Augustus, that a census be taken of all the inhabited earth.

In the very period we have just looked at, Jesus arrived on the scene. Within a matter of years the gospel was racing throughout the Empire. Did the message have any implications for the family? Absolutely! In Appendix II you'll see just how challenging it proved to be.

II.

Paul's Fresh Alternative

Perhaps you've looked at a map in the back of a Bible that traces the apostle Paul's missionary journeys. The cities he visited appear as mere dots on the page. Unfortunately, that's all they are to most of us. Or we may imagine them as dusty, one-horse towns with a few yokels parading around in tunics.

Nothing could be further from the truth. Most of these cities were major commercial, political, intellectual, and religious centers intimately connected with the capital, Rome.

Antioch, for instance—where followers of Christ were first called "Christians"—was the third largest city in the Empire, with a population between 500,000 and one million.

Ephesus was a major tourist center, not unlike Orlando, Florida. In fact, it grew so wealthy by attracting religious pilgrims to the temple of Diana that the leaders opened the first world bank.

Corinth was the most "modern" of the Roman cities, not unlike a planned community today. Less than a hundred years old when its first church began, this beautiful metropolis was favored by the emperors as a site for personal building projects.

It was to these important cities that Paul traveled with the gospel. They certainly needed it! Rome's power and influence, along with her decadent culture, dominated these urban centers, helping to unravel the family bond, particularly among the wealthy. By the time of Christianity, marriage had undergone profound and radical changes, bearing an uncomfortable resemblance to the situation we see in our own culture today.

PAUL'S COUNTER-CULTURAL MESSAGE

All of which brings us to a crucial point: When the New Testament writers addressed the topic of marriage, they weren't simply restating the marriage traditions of their day. Neither were they attempting to revive a form of marriage from the past that had fallen by the wayside. Instead, they were presenting a distinctive, alternative view of the marriage relationship, one that took *courage* to proclaim in light of prevailing trends.

Do you know why that's important? Because people today have a lot of misperceptions about the culture in which the New Testament is rooted. As a result, they misinterpret the Bible's teaching. On the other hand, when they see Scripture against the backdrop of its true cultural context, they gain a radically new perspective on its powerful message. This is particularly true when it comes to what the New Testament says about marriage.

For instance: One modern view is that Paul's teaching on marriage was nothing more than a reflection of first-century culture. Some people even doubt the divine inspiration of his words, saying that they were merely culturally induced. If so, his message would have no authority for us today. But as I've tried to show, the evidence doesn't support that view. Whatever Roman marriage had degenerated into by the time of Paul, it certainly wasn't the institution described in Ephesians 5!

I have little doubt that many couples in Ephesus, Corinth, Rome, Athens, and Antioch were outraged at Paul's marriage instructions and pronouncements—just as many "sophisticated" couples are today. Perhaps they labeled him a Jewish chauvinist. Perhaps they accused him of conspiring with Caesar Augustus to take family life back to the authoritarian days of the patriarchal family. Whatever they said, I'm convinced Paul took a lot of abuse for his marriage proclamations.

But for those who listened closely, Paul's teaching offered

something fresh, unique, fair, and yet radical. It came unexpectedly as a light in the midst of growing moral darkness. It had the
unmistakable ring of inspired truth. And in the end, it prevailed.

One thing is sure: Paul wasn't just parroting the cultural line on
marriage! When we consider what sort of world he came from and
wrote to, we have to admire him and his courage.[1] His message
probably didn't win him any more popularity contests then than it
does now. But, of course, that was not his objective. Instead, along
with the other New Testament writers, Paul was driven to proclaim
the gospel of Jesus Christ to his world, as well as the implications
of that truth for everyday life, including marriage.

RELIABLE GUIDELINES

It is extremely important here that we set the record straight about
marriage and family life in the New Testament world. That's
because as we examine the Bible's teaching on roles, I don't want
there to be any doubts as to the *origin* or authority of the Scripture.
The words may be 2,000 or more years old, but they are inspired
by God, and their message is not bound by culture.

That's a tremendous relief because our world, like Paul's, is
mad with change. We don't need a perspective on life based on
cultural norms; the cultural norms are in upheaval! No, we need
dependable, permanent guidelines with which to build solid marriages and families.

That's exactly what the Bible offers—dependable, permanent
guidelines. Its view of marriage is consistent, reliable, and based
on something infinitely trustworthy: the very character of God
Himself. My wife, Sherard, and I came to believe in the biblical
model of marriage as a young couple in the late sixties and seventies, and we maintained our belief in it throughout the eighties and
now into the nineties. For us, it has proven again and again to be
workable, profitable, trustworthy, fair, and fulfilling.

I hope that's the message you're taking away from this book:
That God's blueprint for building strong, lasting marriages is
appropriate for us to follow today and for our children to follow
tomorrow. It's timeless.

Questions and Answers

Most of the ideas in this book have been presented to hundreds of couples at regional Family Life Seminars and at Fellowship Bible Church in Little Rock, Arkansas. One disadvantage of putting this material in a book is that I don't get to meet you, the reader, face to face. If I could, I bet that you would have any number of questions you'd like to ask me, just as couples in my church or at the seminars come up afterward and barrage me with questions in response to what I've said. I welcome that because every couple's situation is unique. No sermon or book can anticipate and answer every situation.

In this chapter, I want to respond to some of the common questions I'm asked, as well as a few uncommon but interesting questions that provide further insight into the Bible's teaching on roles.

> ■ *You've said that the husband's role is to be the "head" or leader in the marriage, and the wife's is "helping" or nurturing. How, then, should a couple make decisions? Should the husband make all the major ones?*

I understand what you're asking, but the way the question is stated presupposes the idea of a superior/inferior relationship that is to some degree adversarial. As I've tried to show, biblical roles in marriage have to do with responsibility, not rank.

When the Bible assigns the leadership role to the husband, I believe it places on him the primary responsibility of making sure that he and his wife arrive at good decisions, ones that honor God. (By the way, this is where Adam came up short with his wife, Eve.) It doesn't mean the husband must make all the decisions. He can't! He can't be on top of every situation. There are many things his wife knows far more about than he does, making her more qualified to make the decision. Both partners must make independent choices every day. Still, the burden of making sure the family is on a godly course is his. He, not she, is called to bear this weight.

Remember that Adam, not Eve, is charged with the fall of the first family, even though Eve sinned first. I have often wondered what would have happened if Adam had corrected Eve instead of joining with her.

Obviously, major decisions will demand the husband's special attention. To leave these things solely to his wife is irresponsible. It's an abdication of his leadership. It's also unbiblical because God has given him the responsibility of oversight. He must be involved because God's call on him is to be involved. As I said, he bears the burden of making sure that he and his wife arrive at godly choices.

■ *How can a husband determine what the "right" or "godly" decision is?*

In evaluating a decision, the husband should start with the other major player in the relationship—his wife. Why do you think God calls her a "helper" in Genesis 2? God knows that a man doesn't always make good decisions, so He gives him a wife to provide counsel, insight, wisdom, and reaction. He's wise to pay attention to what she says; he's a fool if he ignores it.

When a couple faces a major decision—say, a major purchase or change in direction—they ought to sit down and get all the issues and all the data out on the table. The husband ought to draw out his wife on her feelings, her opinions, and her alternatives, as well as make his own perspective known. That's fulfilling his leadership role. He should also make sure they consider what Scripture has to say, what principles apply to the situation. Of course, they need to pray and ask God for wisdom. Then they need to make the best choice they can.

■ *What happens if a husband and wife discuss and pray about a decision, but they just can't agree? Should the husband go ahead and make the decision, even if his wife is opposed to it?*

Absolutely not! The situation you're describing is what some people refer to as the "dreaded moment of final decision." Who gets to make the call, ultimately? Who owns 51 percent of the stock? Who has superior rank? But you see, that *view* of things operates from an adversarial framework. That's not a biblical framework, by any means.

Let's go back to the principle of the husband as a servant-leader in the pattern of Christ. He comes to an impasse with his wife over some major issue. One thing a Christlike leader, responsible for good decision-making, could do would be to call a timeout and bring in some outside, unbiased counsel. He does this because he wants to be right in the decision, not to win over his wife. Proverbs 11:14 promises, "Where there is an abundance of counselors, there is victory." Because he and his wife can't get unity, they would be wise to turn to outside help and support. It's available. In most cases it can help them move past the logjam they're in.

By the way, I have to say that if a couple has set up their marriage along biblical guidelines, they rarely come to the point where the husband feels he has to make "the infamous final decision" over the objections of his wife. Of course, I do see it in relationships that are adversarial to begin with. But when a man takes responsibility for good decision-making and considers and esteems the input of his wife, they almost never end up in total disagreement—at opposite ends of the spectrum. This certainly has been the case in my home, and many I know.

■ *Are there decisions that a wife should make indepen-*
dently? Are there any that a husband should make inde-
pendently?

Sure, there are hundreds every day! My wife is a person in her own right. She has to take responsibility for herself, and I can't (and don't want to) tell her what to do at every moment. The same holds true for me. The thing to remember is that marriage is an organization, a symbiotic relationship, and both partners have important responsibilities to carry out. Once a working framework and clear roles have been established (and the Bible helps us do that), both husband and wife should be making all kinds of independent decisions, yet always within the framework of these guidelines.

For instance, in our family I handle the bills and record keeping, as I've mentioned. But I've learned that it's important for Sherard to have some control over our income, too. So we set aside a portion of our money for which she has primary responsibility. She makes all kinds of decisions on what to do with that money, independent of me. And I trust her in those decisions.

The choices that marriage partners should not make independently are the ones that involve implications for the marriage or family itself. Whenever a decision affects more than you as an individual, you need to involve the others in the decision-making process.

■ *I agree that the husband should be the leader in a mar-*
riage. But what about men who simply aren't leaders?
What about the fellow who is shy or compliant, or is just
weaker than his wife? What about the wimp?

There are a couple of ways to look at leadership. Some people are just natural leaders. They are inspiring, articulate, visionary, decisive. They're the movers and shakers of the world. They have what it takes to lead an organization, a company, a nation, or whatever. But when it comes to leadership in the home, I don't think that's what the Bible is describing.

From the Bible's perspective, a leader in the home is the man who *accepts responsibility* for his family—to love, provide for, and protect them and to direct them along biblical guidelines. Given that, I believe *every* man can be a leader, *regardless of his personality.* He can do it even if he lacks the inspiration, articulation, and vision of the natural leader. Leadership of the family as a core responsibility is within the grasp of every man.

Of course, a man may not know what that kind of biblical leadership looks like, or even that he is to exercise it. He may be ignorant of it. Or he may not understand exactly how to do it. Or he may just reject it out of disobedience to God. This is where the church can help, by challenging husbands with their God-given responsibility and training them in how they should carry it out.

■ *What about women who exceed their husbands in leadership capacity? What should they do?*

I think you're asking about a wife who is a natural leader. Certainly that is the case in some homes. But just because a wife is a natural leader doesn't mean that she should take over her husband's core responsibilities. She can use her leadership gifts to carry out the role that God has given her as a wife and a mother. And, of course, she can exercise leadership in the community, including at work (as long as she fulfills her responsibilities to her family). But it would be a misuse of her natural abilities if she were to function as the "head" of the marriage. Her job is to help her husband be the man God wants him to be.

I've known a number of women who were natural leader-types and who ended up running their families. I have never seen one who really liked what she got. I believe if any man doesn't feel his wife's support in bearing overall responsibility for the family, *it destroys his sense of manhood.* He will feel humiliated, whether he expresses it or not. He will never be happy, and his wife will never be happy. A woman would be better off using her natural leadership abilities to help her husband carry out his role.

■ *What happens in a marriage when one partner won't live up to his or her biblically defined role? What should the other partner do?*

That question asks about a situation that is all too common, I'm afraid. In millions of homes across North America, even in many Christian homes, people are choosing not to follow the clear direction of Scripture.

The place to begin, of course, is for the partner who recognizes that something is wrong to speak up. With gentleness and sensitivity, he or she needs to point out that there is a problem, and firmly request that the partner act responsibly. This can even be done more than once. However, the direction of this question may assume that such a request has already taken place. Then what? What if there is stubborn resistance, or the offending partner just blows it off? Then there are two additional courses of action.

First, if the issue is relatively minor, such as not picking up after oneself or not being able to balance the checkbook, then I think Scripture counsels against nagging and urges patience and perseverance. In other words, you should do right yourself and remain silent. First Peter 2:19 addresses the relationship between slaves and masters, but I think it offers a principle of "righteous suffering" that carries over into any relationship where one person refuses to behave properly:

> For this finds favor, if for the sake of conscience toward God a man bears up under sorrows when suffering unjustly. For what credit is there if, when you sin and are harshly treated, you endure it with patience? But if when you do what is right and suffer for it you patiently endure it, this finds favor with God.

However, this silence only applies to minor issues. A very different approach is called for when something major is at stake. Suppose one partner is not merely acting irresponsibly, but actually committing overt sin: They're not just sloppy in handling the checkbook, they're defrauding a business. Or they're having an affair. Or they're abusing their wife or husband. Or they're physically or sexually abusing a child. Situations like these call, not for passivity, but for very aggressive action.

It begins with confrontation, and if there is still no response, goes on to exposure. If you are a partner to someone behaving like that, you need to approach a counselor or the proper authorities and report what is going on, and ask for help. I wrote about that in part 7. Unfortunately, on some occasions a partner who seeks help is told to suffer in silence, even though things have reached the point where someone needs to step in. That's an abuse of Scripture. The situation calls for tough love, not passive, enabling silence.

■ *What if one partner is not a believer?*

First Peter 3:1-2 addresses this very thing. The specific context has to do with a believing wife and an unbelieving husband:

> In the same way, you wives, be submissive to your own hus-
> bands so that even if any of them are disobedient to the word
> they may be won without a word by the behavior of their
> wives, as they observe your chaste and respectful behavior.

The phrase "disobedient to the word" is used six other times in Scripture, and in every case it refers to an unbeliever (that is, 1 Peter 2:8). The point is that if your husband is an unbeliever, your best strategy is not to preach at him, but to be silent and do your job, to model "chaste and respectful"—Christlike—behavior. By God's grace, you may eventually win him over to the Lord. I think the same principle applies to a believing husband and an unbelieving wife.

Still, this passage is not talking about violent, addictive, illegal, or immoral behavior. When those kinds of things are taking place, then the believing partner must take appropriate steps of tough love, seeking help and intervention in order to protect herself and her children, and perhaps even to protect the partner from himself.

■ *Robert, you staunchly advocate full-time mothers for
younger children. Does that mean you also advocate government and businesses making it easier on mothers who
have to work?*

The question asks about mothers and young children, but it is not just young children who need a woman's presence and nurture.

Older children and husbands need her, too. I don't believe a woman's employment should be at the expense of her core role as a support system for her husband and children.

In the Persian Gulf War, for every soldier on the battlefield the Allied forces had thirteen support personnel to make him or her effective. In a similar way, I believe that for every person in the public workplace who is putting in an eight-, ten-, or twelve-hour day, we need at least one support person at home to re-energize, encourage, and nurture that worker. We have forgotten that and are paying a dear price for it. People are under tremendous stress nowadays; but a lot of it is because they have absolutely no support system in place at home. Instead they have a partner who is also trying to hold down a full-time job, and who is just as stressed out.

God knew from the beginning that work would prove tiring and demanding, and that workers would need a support system. That seems to be the role He has given to the wife, at least at the core.

Her support role lasts for a lifetime. So even after her kids grow up, having benefited from her full-time mothering, if she decides to re-enter the workforce, she still needs to consider whether she'll have the time and energy to be of support to her husband.

The world being as it is—an information society like ours— women are going to be in the workplace, and we need to accept that reality. Knowing that, and knowing that every worker needs a support system, it would be great if our society would acknowledge that and adjust accordingly. I suppose that would mean government passing laws that would make it easier for women with children to work, and businesses adjusting to the new realities.

There are any number of strategies that could help diminish the tension we now have between work and family. For instance, a company could allow mothers of young children to work mini-workdays, spending four hours a day on the job, and then having the rest of their time to devote to their families. Why does it have to be eight- or even ten-hour days? That would make a big statement about the value placed on children and mothering. It would also be an alternative for some women to having to quit work completely.

Another helpful strategy is providing maternity leave. Women can use their skills productively until they have children, and then for a period of about six to ten years, they could stay at home to rear those children. When they are ready to re-enter the workforce, government or business could put them through a program to bring their skills up to date. They could then go back to work, perhaps starting out part-time and eventually moving to full-time employment.

We can find any number of ways to allow women to work and still maintain their family responsibilities if we just set our minds to it. But in doing so, we must preserve the absolute truth that children need a full-time nurturer when they are young. Scripture says that the person called to that role is the mother.

■ *It sounds nice to say that a woman should be able to rely on a man to support her. But I feel like I'd be taking a big risk to do that, especially when more than 50 percent of all marriages today end in divorce. Shouldn't I at least have some sort of job or career I could fall back on, even if I'm not the main breadwinner for the family? Otherwise, what will I do if my husband ever leaves me, or if he dies prematurely?*

That question reveals the low estate to which marriage has fallen today. You see, *the basic building block of marriage is trust.* If a woman enters the relationship saying, "I have to have a career so I won't have to trust my husband," she's undercutting the very heart of the marriage to begin with.

Still, I think a woman in today's society should prepare herself for more than just childrearing. She would be wise to develop a marketable skill. In fact, as she moves into society and the first season of her marriage, she may use that skill to get her marriage off to a good start.

Later on, she may not need to be employed, and should not if she has young children. But when her kids are grown, she may want to use that skill again in the marketplace. Or she could use it in a volunteer way. God has given her talents and abilities and wants her to develop and use them responsibly. But I don't think He intends her to "hedge her bet" on the possibility that her husband may bail out of the relationship.

> ■ *My father used the same argument you've made in this book—that a woman's place is at home with kids—to avoid paying for my college education, even though he gave my brothers a lot of financial help. I had to foot the bill entirely on my own—and without his blessing! The irony is that I am now a successful executive at a bank (raising two daughters as well) while one of my brothers is divorced and bankrupt, and the other is floundering around trying to find himself, having been in and out of several jobs since college. What's your response to this?*

I'm sorry that your father treated you that way. I do not agree with him in favoring the education of males over females. Every person, every boy or girl, needs to develop their God-given skills as best they can. God wants us to use our abilities to provide for ourselves, to meet the needs of people, and ultimately to love and honor Him. *A woman's contribution to society goes far beyond her home.*

By the way, I don't think I've said that a woman's place is in the home. That would be a comprehensive statement of confinement. It would imply that that was all a woman should do. Nothing could be further from the truth. I purposely chose the word *core* in describing a woman's role *within marriage* so that it would *not* be considered comprehensive, that is, all a woman does. I would feel misrepresented if anyone said I was arguing that "a woman's place is in the home."

> ■ *It's fine to say that a family should live on one income. But my wife would never be satisfied living on what I could make alone. What can I do?*

If your wife truly feels that way, then I suggest that her dissatisfaction may indicate a spiritual problem. God desires that we seek contentment with what He gives us, not dissatisfaction over what we don't have. He doesn't want us craving for more because that amounts to greed and leads to all kinds of problems (see 1 Timothy 6:9-10).

There's little that you can do to change your wife's perspective. She has to make that change. But it may be that she lacks a big picture of the seasons of marriage. She may feel that she's going to have to make do with one income for the rest of her life, and feel insecure about that, or disappointed in light of goals and dreams that you share. I would remind her that nothing in Scripture prohibits two incomes before or after children, so long as she fulfills her responsibilities toward you and your children.

One thing I can guarantee: If she ignores her core responsibilities at home in order to bring in that second income, she will only repeat the same mistake so many *men* have made toward their families. You and your children will slowly but surely resent her for neglecting you. She may gain material things, but what are they worth if she loses her family in the process?

■ *Doesn't your idea of a family living on just the man's income promote overwork on the part of the man?*

Not necessarily. It all depends on the man, on the woman, and on their material expectations. If anything leads to overwork, it's the vision of the American Dream that has been promoted constantly through the media and advertising. In countless ways it stokes the fires of discontent, so that a man works harder and harder to obtain it.

By contrast, I'm suggesting that a man needs to be told from early childhood that an honorable goal for his life is to provide for his wife and family. That's a high and holy calling the Scripture endorses. It's a calling to responsibility, and frankly, to limits, too. That's what we should be instilling in our sons. Instead, too many of us are telling them that they can go out and work and do whatever they want to do, and if they can't make ends meet, their wife's income will make up the difference.

By the way, there are plenty of people who already provide more than enough for their families, and they still work themselves to death. Again, that can indicate a spiritual problem. Invariably it means avoiding one's core role responsibilities.

■ *I'm an employer, and I'd be out of business if I had to rely on men alone for my job pool. How would you address my situation?*

I don't think anyone is suggesting that you go out of business. Scripture never prohibits women from working outside the home. And there are millions of single women who make *valuable* contributions to the workplace. But Scripture does suggest some priorities in life. One of them is that God calls a mother to provide a healthy home for her children. That means she needs to be a helper and nurturer to them. She also needs to be of support to her husband. She should not neglect or violate those priorities.

She may work around them. There are many creative options for women's employment right now, and more on the way. There are also seasons in her family life, as I've shown, and employment is more appropriate in some seasons than in others. Without question, women are going to work in an information society. In some areas, they're going to provide our best workers.

■ *I'm an employer, and I feel just the opposite of the other guy. I feel that women ought to stay home. I'd never admit it publicly, but I'd hire a man over a woman any day, even if the woman's better qualified. Because as soon as you hire a woman, she quits to have a baby. It just ends up costing me a lot of money. Of course, once they get past that stage, that's a different matter. How do you respond to that?*

I can see that you're looking at things realistically, in that it does take a lot of training to bring any new employee up to a productive level. If that employee happens to be a young woman, I can see why you might not want to invest in her when there's a risk she might quit to have a baby.

But I can't agree with the way you allow that to affect your hiring policies. It's not your job to enforce the roles of men and women in their homes by the way you hire at your business. You should be hiring on the basis of competence and skill, and leave the issue of roles and what women and men choose to do in their homes to them. As you've described it, you're practicing a form of job discrimination, which is not only illegal, it's unethical.

You do raise a point that our society needs to come to terms with, though. Government and employers are going to have to devise ways for women to have pregnancy leave, job flexibility, and other means of balancing work and family responsibilities. Much of this is especially important for women who are single parents. The workforce needs to recognize the unique problems women are facing today and compensate for those.

But if I were a young working woman, I wouldn't hold my breath waiting for those changes to happen. Employers have to live by the bottom line, and most who can't provide those kinds of options are going to tend to hire people they think will be reliable for the long-term.

ENDNOTES

Chapter 2—The Myth of the Roleless Marriage

1. Ann Blackman, "Equality," *Time,* Fall 1990, page 14.
2. "More Single Dads, Childless Couples," *Wall Street Journal,* November 12, 1990, page 1B.
3. Blackman, page 13.
4. Eugene H. Fram and Joel Axelrod, "The Distressed Shopper," *American Demographics,* October 1990, pages 44-45.
5. Julia Lawlor, "The New Breadwinner," *Working Mother,* June 1997, page 12.
6. Charles Whited, "Roper Report Shows a Deep and Troubling Rift Between the Sexes," *Miami Herald,* date and page unknown.
7. Dr. James Dobson and Gary Bauer, *Children at Risk* (Dallas, TX: Word, 1990), page 113.
8. Arlie Hochschild, *The Second Shift: Working Parents and the Revolution at Home* (New York: Viking Penguin, Inc., 1989), pages 3-4.
9. "People Patterns," *Wall Street Journal,* October 30, 1989, page B1.
10. Lisa Thatcher, "His & Hers (But Mostly Hers)," *Dallas Morning News,* November 1, 1990, page 1C.

11. Roper poll financed by Philip Morris USA in the name of its Virginia Slims cigarettes, July 22–August 12, 1990; reported in "Women Frustrated With Men," *Dallas Morning News,* April 26, 1990, page 6A.
12. Hochschild, pages 200-201. See pages 15-16 for her definitions of "traditional," "transitional," and "egalitarian" couples.
13. Hochschild, page 19.
14. George Orwell, *Animal Farm* (New York: Harcourt, Brace and Co., 1946).

Chapter 3—Why the Roleless Marriage Won't Work
1. Jill Smolowe, "When Jobs Clash," *Time,* September 3, 1990, page 83.
2. Stephen Clark, *Man and Woman in Christ* (Ann Arbor, MI: Servant Books, 1980), pages 413-414.
3. Sherry B. Ortner, "Is Female to Male as Nature Is to Culture?" *Woman, Culture, and Society,* eds. Michelle Z. Rosaldo and Louise Lamphere (Stanford, CA: Stanford University Press, 1974), pages 67, 70. It's worth noting that Dr. Ortner has pursued her research in hopes of seeing "a genuine change come about, the emergence of a social and cultural order in which as much of the range of human potential is open to women as is open to men."
4. See Joan Bamberger, "The Myth of Matriarchy: Why Men Rule in Primitive Society," *Woman, Culture, and Society,* page 266. Bamberger also says that a few researchers have attempted to prove that cultures exist or once existed in which women ruled rather than men. But this idea turns out to be an unsubstantiated myth (page 263).
5. I know that some people quote Galatians 3:28 as proof that Paul eventually eliminated gender distinctions: "There is neither Jew nor Greek, there is neither slave nor free man, there is neither male nor female; for you are all one in Christ Jesus." But the context clearly shows that this text is talking about salvation in Christ, *not marriage.*

Furthermore, it could just as easily be argued that Galatians 3:28 actually *reinforces* gender distinctions by classifying the groups and then referring to them collectively as "all." Think about it: in the United States we commonly refer to African-Americans, Anglos, Hispanics, Jews, Protestants, Catholics, middle class, lower class, underclass, blue-collar, white-collar, gold-collar, and countless other demographic categories. But we are *all* Americans, with constitutionally guaranteed equal standing before the law. The Constitution does not eliminate these distinctions. It can't; in fact, it offers equal protection and opportunity that would otherwise be denied. The same principle is at work here in Galatians 3:28.

Chapter 4—Reflections on the Traditional Family
1. George H. Gallup Jr. and Dr. Frank Newport, "Parenthood: The American Dream," *Dallas Morning News,* June 4, 1990, page C1.
2. Erma Bombeck, *Motherhood, the Second Oldest Profession* (New York: McGraw-Hill Book Co., 1983), pages 9-13.
3. God places a high value on work. He Himself is a worker and has created people in His image to be His coworkers. For a complete discussion of this issue see *Your Work Matters to God* by Doug Sherman and William Hendricks (Colorado Springs, CO: NavPress, 1987).
4. Samuel Osherson, *Finding Our Fathers* (New York: The Free Press, 1986), page 4.
5. In fact, Dr. James Dobson of Focus on the Family has produced a video special entitled "Where's Dad?" in which he discusses the absence of fathers and the impact of that loss on children.
6. Sheldon Vanauken, *A Severe Mercy* (San Francisco, CA: Harper & Row, Publishers, 1977), page 29.

Chapter 5—Searching for the Biblical Ideal
1. See, for instance, Proverbs 31:10-31; Ephesians 5:21-33; Titus 2:4-5; and1 Peter 3:1-7.

Chapter 6—The High Calling of Headship
1. Lisa Schlein, "New Swiss Marriage Law Ends Men's Reign

as Head of House," *The Atlanta Journal,* January 1988, page 2.

2. For an analysis of the use of the Greek word translated "head" (*kephale*) see Wayne Grudem, "Does *KEFALE* ("Head") Mean 'Source' or 'Authority Over' in Greek Literature?: A Survey of 2,336 Examples," *Trinity Journal,* 6 NS (1985), pages 38-59.

Grudem studied 2,336 instances of the word *kephale* ("head") as used by thirty-six authors from the eighth century B.C.E. to the fourth century A.C.E. He found that in the vast majority of cases (2,034, or 87 percent), the word *kephale* referred to "an actual physical head of a man or animal. The other uses are all metaphorical in some sense or another." He believes that of the remaining instances, forty-nine (only 2.1 percent of the entire sample, but 16.2 percent of the metaphorical uses) refer to a person of superior rank (a ruler); sixty-nine (3 percent of the entire sample, but 22.8 percent of the remaining uses) refer to the starting point in a series; and no instances refer to source or origin.

Helpful as Grudem's analysis is, though, it is inconclusive in determining what Paul means by *kephale* in Ephesians 5 and 1 Corinthians 11. Everyone agrees that Paul uses *kephale* metaphorically in these passages. But by definition, metaphors invite a somewhat subjective interpretation. Whether Paul intends the term to mean an authoritative ruler, or the first in a series, leader, servant-leader, or some other sense of "head" is left open to debate. Of course, one important way of determining a metaphor's meaning is to check the surrounding context. Context along with other biblical references strongly suggest the servant-leader interpretation, in the authors' opinion.

3. Gary Larson, *In Search of the Far Side* (New York: Universal Press Syndicate Company, 1980).

Chapter 9—Feminine Understanding

1. Kevin Cowherd, "Buying Gifts for Women Can Be a Risky Business," *Arkansas Democrat,* April 11, 1989, page 4E.

2. William F. Harley, Jr., *His Needs, Her Needs* (Old Tappan, NJ: Fleming H. Revell Company, 1986), page 11.

Chapter 10—What Every Wife Needs to Succeed

1. Julia Lawlor, "The New Breadwinner," *Working Mother,* June 1997, page 12.
2. I say "biblically" because passages like 2 Thessalonians 3:6-15 and 1 Timothy 5:8 teach this in extremely strong terms.
3. Roper poll financed by Phillip Morris USA in the name of its Virginia Slims cigarettes, July 22–August 12, 1990; reported in "Women Frustrated with Men," *Dallas Morning News,* April 26, 1990, page 6A.
4. John Gray, *Men Are from Mars, Women Are from Venus* (San Francisco: HarperCollins, 1992), p. 137.

Chapter 11—What's a Woman to Choose?

1. Michelle Healy, "Busy Women Let Housework Slide but Not Jobs," *USA Today,* February 25, 1989, page 1.

Chapter 12—Husband-Lover and Child-Lover

1. Elsewhere Scripture affirms that woman enjoys all the rights of man spiritually. She has equal access to all the spiritual blessings and inheritances that man does. In Christ, she has the same standing before God.
2. Passages where the Hebrew word *ezer* is used include: Genesis 2:18,20; Exodus 18:4; Deuteronomy 33:7,26; Psalm 20:2, 70:5, 124:8, 146:5; Isaiah 30:5; Ezekiel 12:14; Daniel 11:34; and Hosea 13:9. See also note 9 below.
3. See Deuteronomy 33:29; Psalm 33:20, 115:9-11.
4. See Psalm 89:19-21.
5. By the way, the same idea carries over into the New Testament, where we find that not only is God the Father a helper, but God the Son is (Hebrews 4:16, 13:6), and God the Holy Spirit is as well (John 14:16, Romans 8:26).
6. Obviously, not all women are able to have children, nor are all women called to be mothers. Those women can still serve God and live productively.
7. Beth Spring, "Who's Minding the Kids?" *Focus on the Family* magazine, April 1989, page 5.

8. Ken Magid and Carol McKelvey, *High Risk: Children Without Conscience* (New York: Bantam, 1987), pages 143, 282. Though childcare experts cited in *High Risk* say two years, this is probably an understated minimum. As a parent of four and a counselor, I believe children need much more than just two years of concentrated attention. The number is surely much higher. Nevertheless, I recommend *High Risk* to any parent who wants the facts about child development and the decisive role parents play.

9. The myth, of course, is that the opportunities won't be there. Some people argue that a woman who leaves her career, bears and raises children, and tries to re-enter the work force puts herself at a real disadvantage. To some extent, that's true. After a ten- or fifteen-year hiatus she will almost certainly return to a workplace in which the nature of the work itself will have changed. And her seniority and experience will have lost much of its value in that new climate.

   Yet that is only half the story. Changes in the workplace will actually work to her advantage because it means new jobs and new opportunities. Furthermore, stepping off the career ladder does not necessarily mean a step backward, even if it feels that way, but rather a postponement of acting on opportunities that will always be there. All the indications are that women will have more opportunities ten or twenty years from now, not less.

   One other angle is too easily overlooked. The one opportunity that will almost certainly not be available to a thirty-five-year-old woman fifteen or twenty years later is the chance to bear children. I think many women in their mid- to late-forties are regretting not pursuing that option.

Chapter 13—Getting into a Man's Head

1. Dr. Joyce Brothers, *What Every Woman Should Know About Men* (New York: Ballantine Books, 1981), page 3.

2. Tom Siegfried, "Brains and Sex: Neural Anatomy's Link to Behavior Differs in Males, Females," *Dallas Morning News,* November 26, 1990, page 6D.

Chapter 14—What Every Wife Needs to Know About Her Husband

1. Seymour Fisher, *Understanding the Female Orgasm* (New York: Basic Books, 1973), page 187.
2. George Gilder, *Men and Marriage* (Gretna, LA: Pelican Publishing Company, 1986), page 10.
3. Gilder, page 10.
4. Margaret Mead, *Male and Female* (New York: Dell, 1949), page 168.

Chapter 15—What Every Husband Needs to Succeed

1. Daniel Levinson, *Seasons of a Man's Life* (New York: Ballantine Books, 1978), pages 332-333.

Chapter 16—What Else a Husband Needs to Succeed

1. See Willard Harley, *His Needs, Her Needs* (Grand Rapids, MI: Fleming H. Revell, a division of Baker Book House Company, 1986, 1994), page 74.
2. Harley, page 41.

Chapter 17—The "S" Word

1. See Romans 13:1; Ephesians 5:21; Colossians 3:18; Titus 2:5, 3:1; 1 Peter 2:13,18, and 3:1.
2. A similar pattern can be seen in Ephesians 5:21–6:9 and Colossians 3:17– 4:1.

Chapter 18—The Masculine Counterpart to the "S" Word

1. James C. Dobson, *What Wives Wish Their Husbands Knew About Women* (Waco, TX: Word Books, 1980), page 22.
2. As quoted by W. Peter Blitchington, *Sex Roles and the Christian Family* (Wheaton, IL: Tyndale House, 1980), page 91.

Chapter 22—The Church: Can It Be a Refuge for Women?

1. Kay Marshall Strom, *In the Name of Submission: A Painful Look at Wife Battering* (Portland, OR: Multnomah Press, 1986), page 52.

2. Passages like Matthew 18:15-17, 2 Thessalonians 3:6-15, and 1 Timothy 3:4-5 show that the Church paid attention to what was going on in the homes of its members and was prepared to step in when necessary to enforce justice and protection.
3. Paul told Timothy essentially the same thing in 1 Timothy 4:11-16.
4. See also Titus 1:6-9.
5. Church discipline or at least monitoring is clearly in view in passages such as Matthew 18:15-17, Galatians 6:1-2, 1 Timothy 5:3-16, 2 Thessalonians 3:6-15, and James 5:14-16. The church's authority is upheld in passages like Titus 2:15 and 1 Peter 5:1-5.

Chapter 23—Church Intervention: A Case Study
1. Details in this illustration, including elements of the letter that Cheri wrote to her husband, have been altered to protect identities. However, this is a true story.

Chapter 24—Forget-Me-Nots
1. Quoted by Kathleen Deveny, "Grappling with Women's Evolving Roles," *Wall Street Journal,* September 5, 1990, page B1.
2. Cultures in the biblical world enjoyed a much greater "seamlessness" between work and home. A great deal of the work in the ancient world was conducted in or very near homes, and families themselves were productive economic units. Consequently, the idea of work "outside the home" would have seemed strange.
3. A. Levine, "Second Thoughts About Infant Day Care," *U.S. News and World Report,* May 4, 1987, pages 73-74.
4. Claudia Wallis, "Is Day Care Bad for Babies?" *Time,* June 22, 1987, page 63.
5. Wallis, page 63.
6. Mark Jenkins, "Do You Really Need Two Incomes?" *Men's Health,* April 1998, page 94.
7. "People Patterns," *Wall Street Journal,* November 29, 1990, page B1, reporting on 1988 data from the National Center for

Health Statistics.

8. "Pregnant Women in the Workforce" (table based on Rand Corporation study), "Work Around Childbirth," *Wall Street Journal,* February 6, 1991, page B1.

9. Ken Magid and Carol McKelvey, *High Risk: Children Without Conscience* (New York: Bantam Books, 1987), page 27.

10. Magid and McKelvey, page 27.

11. Magid and McKelvey, page 245.

12. George H. Gallup Jr. and Dr. Frank Newport, "Parenthood: The American Dream," *Dallas Morning News,* June 4, 1990, page C1. According to Gallup, 33 percent would choose a situation in which both parents work and take care of the children equally; only 1 percent would choose a situation in which the father stays home while the mother works.

13. Gallup and Newport, page C1.

14. Lisa Thatcher, "His & Hers (But Mostly Hers)," *Dallas Morning News,* November 1, 1990, page 1C.

15. Grace Mitchell, *The Day Care Book* (New York: Stein and Day, 1979), pages 203-204.

Chapter 25—Seasons of Life

1. See 1 Kings 3:12, 4:29-31.

Chapter 26—Gifting Your Child's Marriage

1. As quoted in Gordon McDonald, *The Effective Father* (Wheaton, IL: Tyndale House, 1977), page 94.

2. Peter Blitchington, *Sex Roles and the Christian Family* (Wheaton, IL: Tyndale House, 1981), page 18.

3. "People Patterns," *Wall Street Journal,* March 3, 1989, page B1.

4. Anastasia Toufexis, "The Lasting Wounds of Divorce," *Time,* February 6, 1989, page 61.

5. "More Single Dads, Childless Couples," *Wall Street Journal,* November 12, 1990, page 1B.

6. George Sweeting, *Great Quotes and Illustrations* (Waco, TX: Word, 1985), page 45.

7. See 2 Peter 2:7.

8. Quoted by Joe White, *Looking for Leadership* (Branson, MO: Operation Challenge, 1984), pages 97-98.
9. John Markle, "Text of McCambridge Letter," *Arkansas Democrat,* April 18, 1989, page 11A.

Appendix I—Roleless Chaos of Another Day

1. Author's loose paraphrase of two translations of Columella, quoted in Lilian Portefaix, *Sisters Rejoice: Paul's Letter to the Philippians and Luke-Acts as Seen by First-Century Philippian Women,* Coniectanea Biblica, New Testament Series 20 (Stockholm, Sweden: Almqvist & Wiskell International, 1988), pages 15,17. The actual translation as presented by Portefaix reads: "For both among the Greeks and afterwards amongst the Romans down to the time which our fathers can remember domestic labour was practically the sphere of the married woman, the fathers of the families betaking themselves to the family fireside, all care laid aside, only to rest from their public activities. For the utmost reverence for them ruled in the home, in an atmosphere of harmony and diligence, and the most beauteous of women was fired with emulation, being zealous by her care to increase and improve her husband's business. No separate ownership was to be seen in the house, nothing which either the husband or the wife claimed by right as one's own, but both conspired for the common advantage, so that the wife's diligence at home vied with the husband's public activities.

   "Nowadays, however, when most women so abandon themselves to luxury and idleness that they do not deign to undertake even the superintendence of wool-making and there is a distaste for home-made garments and their perverse desire can only be satisfied by clothing purchased for large sums and almost the whole of their husband's income, one cannot be surprised that these same ladies are bored by a country estate and the implements of husbandry, and regard a few days' stay at a country house as a most sordid business."
2. Author's loose paraphrase of two translations of Tacitus, quoted in Portefaix, pages 16-17. The actual translation as presented by Protefaix reads: "In the good old days, every

man's son, born in wedlock, was brought up not in the chamber of some hireling nurse, but in his mother's lap, and at her knee. And that mother could have no higher praise than that she managed the house and gave herself to her children.

Again, some elderly relative would be selected in order that to her, as a person who had been tried and never found wanting, might be entrusted the care of all the youthful scions of the same house; in the presence of such an one no base word could be uttered without grave offence, and no wrong deed done. Religiously and with the utmost delicacy she regulated not only the serious tasks of her youthful charges, but their recreations also and their games.

"Nowadays, on the other hand, our children are handed over at their birth to some silly little Greek serving-maid, with a male slave, who may be anyone, to help her—quite frequently the most worthless member of the whole establishment, incompetent for serious service. It is from the foolish tittle-tattle of such persons that the children receive their earliest impressions, while their minds are still green and unformed; and there is not a soul in the whole house who cares a jot what he says or does in the presence of his baby master. Yes, and the parents themselves make no effort to train their little ones in goodness and self-control; they grow up in an atmosphere of laxity and pertness, in which they gradually come to lose all sense of shame, and all respect both for themselves and for other people."

3. The same ruler who ordered the census that took Mary and Joseph to Bethlehem, where Jesus was born (Luke 2:1-4).

4. We see this reflected, for example, in Acts 2:8-11.

5. J.P.V.D. Balsdon, *Roman Women: Their History and Habits* (Westport, CT: Greenwood Press, Publishers, 1962), page 207. Note that spinning and weaving were the exclusive prerogative of women, something in which they took great pride.

6. This century has seen a dramatic increase in research on women of the first century. However, despite an extensive amount of literary and archaeological data, clear and unanimous picture has yet to emerge.

7. Will Durant, *Caesar and Christ* (New York: Simon and Schuster, 1944), page 370.

8. Jérome Carcopino, *Daily Life in Ancient Rome* (New Haven, CT: Yale University Press, 1966), page 85. See also Sarah B. Pomeroy, *Goddesses, Whores, Wives, and Slaves* (New York: Schocken Books, 1965), pages 169-170, 188-189; and Balsdon, page 45.

9. For the following paragraphs see Pomeroy, pages 199-201. See also Durant, page 370.

10. Pomeroy, pages 199-201.

11. See Lilian Portefaix, *Sisters Rejoice,* page 24, n. 115: and Pomeroy, page 200. In this light recall Lydia, "a seller of purple fabrics," one of Paul's first converts in Macedonia (Acts 16:14-15).

12. Balsdon, page 277.

13. Durant, page 363.

14. Carcopino, page 96.

15. Carcopino, page 97.

16. Carcopino, page 100.

17. Carcopino wrote: "To be frank, if the frequency of adultery had diminished in the second century, this ws not due to the intermittent severities of the law but because facilities for divorce had, as it were, legitimised adultery by anticipation" (page 95; see also page 90).

18. Durant, page 370.

19. Carcopino, page 93, citing Juvenal 6, 300-305.

20. Eva Cantarella, *Pandora's Daughters: The Role and Status of Women in Greek and Roman Antiquity* (Baltimore, MD: Johns Hopkins University Press, 1987), page 159.

21. The irony is that Augustus himself died without fathering an heir, as did several of his successors—viz., Tiberius, Caligula, Claudius, and Nero (see Cantarella, page 160).

22. Durant, page 363.

23. Portefaix, pages 9-10: "At the birth of a girl her coming fate was determined by the midwife and by the paterfamilias [the patriarchal head of the family], both of whom had in different ways the authority to decide upon life or death for a newborn

child. It was the task of the midwife to examine the child to assess its physical condition. In those cases where she discovered deformity or obvious weakness the law ordained that the child, whatever its sex, should immediately be killed. If the midwife found a girl capable of survival it was left to the father to determine whether she should be kept in the family or not. When a girl was rejected, it was not, however, a matter of killing her, as was the fate of deformed children. The fact is that the unwanted girls were sold or exposed in much frequented places in the hope of their being rescued, either for mercy or greed. A girl might prove a financial asset as a servant to an innkeeper or the hostess of a brothel, for instance." (See also Cantarella, pages 135-136).

24. Durant, page 364.
25. Judith Waldrop, "You'll Know It's the 21st Century When . . .," *American Demographics*, December 1990, page 23.
26. "People Patterns," *Wall Street Journal,* March 3, 1989, page B1.
27. "People Patterns," page B1.

Appendix II—Paul's Fresh Alternative

1. When we read in Acts and elsewhere of how freely Paul moved among the peoples, cultures, and world-views he encountered, the notion of Paul as a Jewish traditionalist becomes inconceivable. Peter may come close to that description, but not Paul.

Authors

Robert Lewis is the teaching pastor of Fellowship Bible Church in Little Rock, Arkansas. He has written three books on marriage and has been a featured speaker at national and international conferences for Campus Crusade's Family Ministry for eleven years. He is married and has four children.

William Hendricks is a communications consultant for Hendricks Group in Dallas, Texas. William is married and has three daughters. This is his fifth book.

RESOURCES TO STRENGTHEN YOUR HOME

Marriage Takes More Than Love

Marriage is all about choice. Learn how to make choices in your marriage that are best for all three parties involved— you, your spouse, and God.

Marriage Takes More Than Love
(Jack and Carole Mayhall)

Marriage Mender

Marriage is more than just finding the "right" person—it's about working with your spouse even when starting from scratch seems like the best option. If you're looking for a fresh start, this book will give you the solution-based tools you need to rebuild your marriage.

Marriage Mender
(Thomas A. Whiteman, and Thomas G. Bartlett)

Taming the Family Zoo

Does your house sometimes feel more like a zoo than a home? Here's a great tool to help you identify the unique personality type of each of your children and learn ways to adapt your parenting style for each child.

Taming the Family Zoo
(Jim and Suzette Brawner)

To get your copies visit your local bookstore, call 1-800-366-7788 or log on to www.navpress.com. Ask for a FREE catalog of NavPress Products. Offer **#BPA**.

NAVPRESS
BRINGING TRUTH TO LIFE
www.navpress.com